AF526828

SKILLFUL MEANS

BUDDHIST TRADITION SERIES

Edited by

ALEX WAYMAN

VOLUME 54

SKILLFUL MEANS

The Heart of Buddhist Compassion

JOHN W. SCHROEDER

Foreword by

THOMAS P. KASULIS

MOTILAL BANARSIDASS PUBLISHERS
PRIVATE LIMITED • DELHI

First Indian Edition: Delhi, 2004

(First published by the University of Hawai'i Press, 2001
under 'Society for Asian and Comparative Philosophy', Monograph Series No. 18)

ISBN: 81-208-1999-3 (Cloth)
ISBN: 81-208-2002-9 (Paper)

Also available at:
MOTILAL BANARSIDASS
41 U.A. Bungalow Road, Jawahar Nagar, Delhi 110 007
8 Mahalaxmi Chamber, 22 Bhulabhai Desai Road, Mumbai 400 026
236, 9th Main III Block, Jayanagar, Bangalore 560 011
120 Royapettah High Road, Mylapore, Chennai 600 004
Sanas Plaza, 1302 Baji Rao Road, Pune 411 002
8 Camac Street, Kolkata 700 017
Ashok Rajpath, Patna 800 004
Chowk, Varanasi 221 001

Printed in India
BY JAINENDRA PRAKASH JAIN AT SHRI JAINENDRA PRESS,
A-45 NARAINA, PHASE-I, NEW DELHI 110 028
AND PUBLISHED BY NARENDRA PRAKASH JAIN FOR
MOTILAL BANARSIDASS PUBLISHERS PRIVATE LIMITED,
BUNGALOW ROAD, DELHI 110 007

Dedicated,

From the life stream of skin, flesh, bones, and marrow,

To Grace

Contents

Foreword

(by Series Editor)

This book is an interesting application of *Skillful Means,* including compassion, to discussions of Buddhism, whether Hīnayāna or Mahāyāna. Apparently, it was not held as necessary to know the technical meanings of the Buddhist terms; and persons who find it appropriate to know such meanings may not be able to apply *Skillful Means* in the manner employed by Professor John W. Schroeder. So, may I congratulate Schroeder on his discussions using this 'Skillful Means,' and therefore worthy of inclusion in the Buddhist Tradition Series.

—Alex Wayman

Foreword

Rare is the book that challenges us to rethink what we believe we already know and understand. This is just such a book. On one level, John Schroeder is developing a philosophical interpretation of the Buddhist notion of *upāya* or "skillful means," an idea with which any student of Buddhism is probably familiar. Yet, as we read the book, we find that Schroeder has done something more profound and less expected—he has led us to a different way of thinking about Buddhism and what it is all about. He has encouraged us to see Buddhism as not primarily involved in explaining reality and knowledge, but instead as teaching the praxes that lead to such goals as mindfulness or compassion. That is, he argues that what we often take to be Buddhist metaphysics or epistemology are, instead, reflections on and within praxis (so-called "metapraxis"), thereby justifying the procedure of personalizing the teachings for the particular audience at hand. In this new light, *upāya* becomes not so much a doctrine that some Buddhists believe, but rather a name for an enterprise in which all Buddhists are involved in one way or another. Schroeder's thesis, in short, is that Buddhists are less interested in teaching about what reality is than they are in teaching about how we are to find awareness and compassion in our practices, in helping us live our lives skillfully.

To many readers, this might seem not new at all. Even the early commentators on Buddhism in the West, people like D. T. Suzuki, tended to say things like "Buddhism is not a philosophy; it is a way of life." Schroeder's line of argument shows us, however, a better way of putting this. Although

Buddhism is a praxis and a way of life, such a way of life does not exclude philosophy. That is, Buddhism is not a philosophy *as contrasted with* a way of life. Although Buddhism may not be a philosophy as an independent academic discipline, it does not follow that there is no philosophical dimension *within* a Buddhist way of life. At the base of any religion, Buddhism included, is praxis. Typically, there are multiple praxes within any tradition, sometimes emphasized by different subsects of the same tradition. In explaining and justifying the praxes, various philosophical claims and arguments may be made. Such statements are indeed philosophy (Suzuki missed that point), but they are a kind of philosophizing that cannot be separated from the praxes out of which they arise (the insight behind Suzuki's comment). In my own work, I have labeled this form of philosophizing "metapraxis" to contrast it with theories about the nature of reality, "metaphysics." Schroeder has, I believe, used the distinction fruitfully in this book.

We can better grasp the point of Schroeder's emphasis on Buddhist philosophy as metapraxis by considering an analogy from a mundane kind of human experience. As I was walking through the park the other day, I stopped to watch a team of nine-year olds having a baseball practice. The coach was working with the youngsters, helping them in their batting. One girl was very aggressive at the plate, swinging hard and trying to hit a homerun every time. She consistently missed or just barely hit the ball. The coach told her, "Don't try to kill the ball; just let the bat meet the ball." On the next swing, the girl hit a nice line drive into the outfield. "That's it. Now you're getting it." The next kid was a boy who was rather timid at the plate, seemingly afraid of missing the ball and hesitating to take a full swing. The coach yelled out encouragingly, "Don't worry about hitting the ball; just swing away." The lad let it rip on the next swing, missing the ball by at least two inches. The coach chimed out, "That's it. Good. Don't worry about missing. Just keep on swinging." I suspect we can all think of parallel expressions used in various kinds of teaching, whether they be from sports, music performance, dance, crafts, or the arts. They are part of everyday praxis.

Suppose in our little story, however, that I were a die-hard metaphysician (or epistemologist perhaps) who had just witnessed the coach's instructions and approached him after the practice to submit him to some tough-minded questioning. We could imagine a dialogue that might have gone like this:

Metaphysician: "I know that these are just kids, but I don't see why you have to lie to them."

Coach: "I didn't lie. What do you mean?"

M: "Well, you told the girl to let the bat meet the ball and then you told the boy to swing without concern for hitting the ball. Both teachings can't be right because they contradict each other: one says to focus on the ball and bat and the other says to focus on the swing itself without regard for the ball and bat. So, which is right? Because either one or both must be wrong, you're lying to at least one of them. Why?"

C: "I wasn't lying. I was just adjusting what I was saying in response to what I saw in their respective swings. Every kid is different—some are confident, some overconfident, some hesitant, some sticklers for technique, some highly intuitive. Right?"

M: "Sure."

C: "Well, I try to factor that into what I'm saying. I'm interested in results. One way of putting things may work for one kid, but not for another."

M: "Well, how did you know what was wrong in their swings? You must have some idea of a perfect swing that they were not attaining. If so, why don't you just teach them *that?*"

C: "In a way, I am. I mean, if they take to heart my advice and my advice is good, their swings will improve. Eventually, they'll both be swinging the right way. There may be some differences in style between them, but overall, they will have just about the same swing."

M: "So, what you're saying to them is just an expedience, a means to an end. Along the way, you are fudging the truth to get them to the point where you don't have to deceive them any more. I understand your motive, but I am unhappy with it. It seems immoral. You see, I don't believe in telling white lies, however benign the motive. When we start telling untruths, they may be efficacious in some short-term sense, but in the end, they undermine trust in the honesty of others and, maybe even more dangerously, deny the audience's autonomy. The students can never figure out the truth on their own because they depend on the teacher's pedagogical sequence, filled as it is with expeditious white lies. That doesn't seem right to me."

C: "Now wait a minute. I never said I'm telling white lies. I'm just trying to help them become better batters, to be more skillful in what they're trying to do. I'm not pretending to start from scratch. I'm just starting with where they are, jumping into the situation as it presents itself. I'm working with what I've got, what they bring to me. I'm not trying to tell them some kind of absolute truth about the universe; I'm just nudging them along a path that will help them do better what they're trying to do."

M: "Well, maybe. I understand you're trying to help them—I don't in any way question your good intentions. But I still don't see why you just don't teach them the perfect swing and forget all this intermediary distortion of the final goal."

C: "I'm not sure where you're going with this 'final goal' stuff. Maybe I was misleading you when I let you characterize my goal as 'the perfect swing.' There is no 'perfect swing' that can be explained in some unambiguous way. Even if there were such a thing as a 'perfect swing,' I couldn't just explain it to them. They have to feel how it works, not abstractly understand it, and that comes from practicing over and over again with some good supervision. I am helping them to swing more perfectly without having some fixed idea of a preconceived ideal. No two 'perfect swings'—as you call them—are exactly alike. Yet, when I see one, I know it."

M: "Ah, but *how* do you know it? What's the foundation, the verification, of that purported knowledge?"

C: "I just know it. How? Probably because I've played baseball almost all my life and I've watched thousands of batters, good and bad, over the years. I've been coached myself as a batter, and I've coached others. Basically, I learned just the way these kids are learning."

M: "Oh, now I see. You're just passing down a kind of technical know-how. You've got no real knowledge about the way things are; you just have a set of acquired skills, a craft. Truth doesn't even come into play."

C: "If that works for you, I'll accept that. Now, if you'll excuse me, I promised Samantha I'd help her with her swing after practice and she's waiting for me."

M: "Sure thing. Sorry to have taken up your time. I'm a philosopher and I just can't help but ask such questions. I'll let you go. Teach Samantha well—be crafty."

That little dialogue can help us focus on some key points in Schroeder's analysis. First, before the intervention of the metaphysician, the coach was simply involved in the praxis of teaching baseball skills. To the extent he is doing it well and the players improve, his teachings are expedients or "skillful means." In Buddhist terminology, they are *upāya.* In coaching the youngsters, the coach simply responded to the problems each player was having with his or her swing. The situation changed, however, once the metaphysician challenged those teaching practices. The coach then began to reflect on what he was doing and how to justify it. The discussion changed from the practical to the metapractical. The coach was no longer simply practicing coaching, but also analyzing the rationale in his coaching and why its methods are effective. The metaphysician kept missing the point, however, by seeking strict logical coherence in the coach's praxis. The metaphysician wanted the coach to have a single set of instructions or a single paradigm for the perfect swing. In response, the coach tried to explain the fluidity and apparent incoherence in his praxis as coach. The Buddhist justification for *upāya*, Schroeder shows, is similar to that kind of metapraxis.

Furthermore, in our dialogue the coach ends the discussion noting that the philosopher's interpretation may still not be perfect. Yet, at least now the metaphysician has a way of understanding why coaching statements need not have absolute consistency in the strict logical sense. Nor are they about "truth" as typically defined in metaphysics or epistemology. If ever in the position of teaching someone to hit a baseball, that metaphysician would (because of the interpretation developed here) be freer to teach without concern for tight logical consistency. In his own terminology, the metaphysician would be teaching the know-how of a craft instead of the knowing-that of metaphysics or epistemology. In that respect, the coach's metapractical discussion with the metaphysician was also *upāya:* the coach did not insist on defining the one and only, absolute, unqualified metapractical theory of how to coach batting. Instead, he let his interlocutor go off with an understanding that "works for you." By helping the metaphysician realize how metaphysics does not apply in this case, the coach coached the philosopher as well as Samantha.

In this book, John Schroeder shows how much of Buddhist philosophizing can be understood along similar lines. In doing so, he cuts against the grain of much common buddhological scholarship. (1) He shows that the general idea of *upāya,* though not necessarily the term itself, is found in both the Early Buddhism and Abhidharma Buddhism as well as Mahāyāna. (2) He shows that in Mahāyāna sūtras like the *Vimalakīrti* the emphasis and use of narrative is given a metapractical justification of sorts as part of its larger acceptance of the techniques of *upāya.* (3) He argues that

Nāgārjuna's philosophy is best understood as metapractical rather than metaphysical or mystical. That is, Schroeder's view is that Nāgārjuna's arguments are always targeted to a particular audience whose praxes are corrupted by unskillful philosophical theories. By that account, we could say Nāgārjuna is philosophizing, but only in the *upāya*-like metapractical sense, rather than the metaphysical or epistemological sense. Just as the coach used philosophy in talking with a philosopher, Nāgārjuna used philosophical arguments in talking with philosophers, but that in itself does not make either the coach or Nāgārjuna a "philosopher" in some definitive sense. For Nāgārjuna to make philosophy itself a path to skillful practice would be as silly as the baseball coach trying to articulate a "perfect swing." (4) Schroeder articulates a metapractical reason for why Ch'an/Zen and Pure Land Buddhism could be practiced together in some East Asian contexts. If we take the Ch'an/Zen idea of nothingness and the Pure Land idea of Amida's saving grace as metaphysical teachings, there is no room for practicing the two together. However, if we take those teachings to be more metapractical than metaphysical, there *is* room for the practical confluence of the two traditions, just as there is room on a baseball team for different players to follow different instructions in their individual practice.

In summation, through his synoptic vision of the Buddhist tradition, Schroeder shifts our understanding of *upāya* from being a particular doctrine in certain schools of Buddhism to being a way of thinking about praxis found in virtually all schools of Buddhism. For me at least, this suggests that there is nothing wrong in studying Buddhist controversies as philosophical disagreements as long as we remember that they are based in and ultimately about Buddhist praxis. They are always used in particular, not universal, contexts. Nor does Schroeder's approach commit us to saying that all Buddhists agree on philosophical matters. They often disagree, just as coaches may disagree among themselves, but the philosophical point of contention is metapractical, not metaphysical. Metapraxis, like any philosophical enterprise, has restrictions, a need for consistency, for instance. For example, our batting coach might have said seemingly inconsistent things to different players, but his metapractical justification (differences are necessary to adapting the message to the temperament, habits, and readiness of each player) was itself consistent.

John Schroeder has given us a fascinating and provocative study. Even for those who might disagree with some detail in the argument, the overall thesis remains engaging and leads us to a more fruitful level of discussion. Schroeder is urging us to formulate our buddhological and philosophical questions in a new way and in so doing, opens up new vistas on the tradition. Buddhist scholarship itself is, after all, a praxis. Schroeder makes us philosophically reflect on that praxis and thereby makes us more skillful at what we do.

Thomas P. Kasulis

Teacher and disciple practicing mutually is the twining vines of buddha ancestors. Twining vines of buddha ancestors is the life stream of skin, flesh, bones, and marrow. Taking up a flower and winking is twining vines. Breaking into a smile is skin, flesh, bones, and marrow. The seeds of twining vines have the power of dropping away body. Branches, leaves, flowers, and fruit of twining vines do and do not interpenetrate one another. Thus, buddha ancestors appear, and the fundamental point is actualized.

—Dōgen

Acknowledgments

It would be impossible to give thanks to all the people who have helped shaped this book. It has taken many twists and turns, and has been guided by the generous criticisms and intellectual support of many people.

My deepest gratitude goes to my dear friend and mentor Don Levi from the University of Oregon. Don supported this project from its very beginnings, and has read and reread many versions of the manuscript. His genuine concern for my intellectual development, his warm friendship, and his penetrating insights have made this project come to fruition. More than anyone else, he taught me the beauty of what Dōgen means by the "mutual practice of teacher and student."

My sincerest gratitude also goes to Henry Rosemont, Jr. from St. Mary's College of Maryland. Henry offered detailed criticisms and suggestions of the manuscript, and helped me think of the project in relation to the Buddhist traditions of China and Japan. As my professional mentor, he has adopted the role of a true Confucian Master, guiding my development as a teacher and scholar of the "cross-cultural way."

Special thanks also go to Thomas Kasulis from The Ohio State University who pressed me to think hard about the idea of "skillful means." It was during his NEH Seminar on Zen Buddhism in 1997 that I rethought the entire project along the idea of "metapraxis," and he has since read the manuscript carefully, giving helpful criticisms and corrections. I am especially grateful for his willingness to write the foreword.

Besides this, many other people underlie the making of the book. Special thanks to my loving "lotus" friend Lance Popoff who helped revise the first sections of the book; to Stephen Stern for his deep friendship and for his help with the conclusion; to Michael Webb for his undivided love and emotional support; to Larry Rich and Celia Escudero for their inspiration; to Shane Farrell for years of friendship; to Mehmet Gencer for his generosity; to C. T. for helping me put "skillful means" into practice; to Michelle Desailly for offering a warm Australian home to work in; and, of course, to my mother and father who gave me the world.

Special thanks also to St. Mary's College of Maryland for financial support to do research in India; to professor Alan Paskow for financial assistance from the Division of Human Development; to my colleagues in the Department of Philosophy and Religious Studies for providing me with a productive and supportive workspace; to Devin Polster, Jake Karaczynski, and Richard Mroczynski who helped format and index the manuscript; and to Keith K. Leber from the University of Hawai'i Press for his patience and editorial guidance.

Finally, I would like to thank Professor Hee-jin Kim from the University of Oregon who first introduced me to Buddhist philosophy. Without his initial inspiration, this book would have never been written.

A note about the text. While I have tried to remain faithful to the Sanskrit transliteration, I have taken some liberties with a few key words, altering their form for the sake of brevity and cohesion. I have also standardized the text as much as possible, using Sanskrit instead of Pāli in most sections.

SKILLFUL MEANS

Introduction

There is a famous story in the Buddhist Pāli text, the *Mahāvagga,* about the Buddha's initial hesitation to express his teachings to the world. Arising from five weeks of meditation on the nature of suffering and spiritual bondage, it suddenly occurred to the Buddha that his Dharma, which is "deep, difficult to see, difficult to understand, peaceful, excellent, beyond dialectic" might get distorted by a world "cloaked in the murk" of attachments. In fact, given the "habitual tendencies" of most people, the Buddha felt his teachings would only cause more suffering and confusion in the world, and, rather than "tread against the stream" of ignorance and confusion, he thought it would be better to remain silent and not teach about his experiences at all.

If the story stopped here then we would know nothing of the Buddha's teachings. But the Hindu god Brahmā suddenly appeared to the Buddha, urging him to teach. The god knelt at the Buddha's feet and pleaded, "Lord, let the Lord teach *dhamma*, let the Well-farer teach *dhamma*; there are beings with little dust in their eyes who, not hearing *dhamma* are decaying, but if they are learners of *dhamma*, they will grow" (Horner 1962, p. 9). Brahmā repeated his plea three times, and as the Buddha listened he began to see the world in a new light:

> As the Lord was surveying the world with the eye of an awakened one, he saw beings with little dust in their eyes, with much dust in their eyes, with acute faculties, with dull faculties, of good dispositions, of

> bad dispositions, docile, indocile, few seeing fear in sins and the worlds beyond (Horner 1962, p. 9).

In both the *Mahāvagga* and *Majjhima-Nikāya*, the Buddha's vision is compared to various lotus ponds with different degrees of growth:

> Even as in a pond of blue lotuses or in a pond of red lotuses or in a pond of white lotuses, a few blue or red or white lotuses are born in the water, grow in the water, do not rise above the water but thrive while altogether immersed; a few blue or red or white lotuses are born in the water, grow in the water and reach the surface of the water; a few blue or red or white lotuses are born in the water, grow in the water, and stand up rising out of the water, undefiled by the water (Horner 1967, p. 210).

The story then relates the Buddha's vision to the nature of humanity: just as there are various types of lotuses, so there are various stages of human growth, each with different degrees of "dust" and confusion in their minds. Upon seeing these "wondrous" differences, the Buddha knew it would be useless to preach universally or speak as if everyone were the same. He knew that if he wanted to help others he would need to be sensitive to the karmic differences of human beings and mold his teachings to their level. With this new wisdom, the Buddha decided to "Turn the Wheel of Dharma" to his former ascetic companions.

The Mahāyāna tradition in Buddhism sees this story as pivotal because it expresses an intimate relationship between wisdom (*prajñā*) and compassion (*karuṇā*). Rather than saying the Buddha attains enlightenment *before* he hesitates to preach Dharma, the Mahāyānists say his enlightenment culminates in the realization that human beings differ and that he must teach depending on the relative emotional, intellectual, and spiritual dispositions of his audience. They say this not only connects the Buddha's enlightenment to the "everyday" world but reveals the compassionate wisdom of a great bodhisattva who responds to the concrete suffering of others.

This link between wisdom and compassion, called "skill-in-means" (*upāya-kauśalya*) in the Mahāyāṇa tradition, is what this book will explore. Very generally, *upāya* refers to the different pedagogical styles, meditation techniques, and religious practices that help people overcome attachments, and to the ways in which Buddhism is communicated to others. Like the example of the Buddha in the above story, "skillful means" arises from the idea that wisdom is embodied in how one responds to others rather than an abstract conception of the world, and reflects an ongoing concern with the soteriological effectiveness of the Buddhist teachings.

One goal of this study is to chart this view of "skillful means" throughout important moments in Buddhist history. It will focus on the different pedagogical styles that are used in Buddhism, exploring the various ways in which the Dharma is communicated and taught to others. As Michael Pye notes, Western scholars generally neglect this approach to Buddhism:

> It is fair to say that the method of thought and practice summed up by the concept of skilful means is one of the fundamental principles of Buddhism. And yet, strangely enough the matter has never been the subject of extended study....'Nirvāṇa', 'bodhisattva', 'emptiness',

> and so on have all been considered in this way and that, but apart from occasional references and brief definitions 'skilful means' has scarcely been attended to at all. A concept which has been used to explain the very existence of Buddhism as a functioning religious system demands closer attention (Pye 1978, p. 1).

Pye's examination of *upāya* is primarily a textual analysis of "skilful means" in the *Lotus Sūtra* and the *Perfection of Insight* literature, and, while it does offer some suggestive insights about the philosophical implications of *upāya*, it offers little in the way of a critical approach to Buddhist philosophy. The focus of this book points to a larger, critical issue in the Buddhist tradition. Simply put, there are some Buddhist traditions (such as the Abhidharma) that say the Buddha established basic meditative practices for all Buddhists to follow, and that some of his teachings are therefore "absolutely" true; and there are other traditions (such as the early Mahāyāna) that say all the Buddha's teachings are none other than "skill-in-means." While the Abhidharma Buddhists say the Buddha sometimes taught "conventional" (*samvṛtti*) or "skillful" doctrines for the ignorant, they also say he established a universal path, or *mārga*, in his "ultimate" teachings (*paramārtha*). For the Mahāyāna, however, to say the Buddha established a definitive soteriological path constricts his teachings into a fixed remedy and drains them of compassion.

The doctrine of *upāya* mirrors this debate, and refers to a critical, self-reflective movement in the Buddhist tradition. The bulk of Western Buddhist scholarship ignores this critical element by focusing either on the philosophical implications of certain Buddhist terms like "non-self," "emptiness," and "buddha-nature," or by focusing exclusively on Buddhist religious praxis. This methodological split generally pits philosophers on one side who explore the metaphysical, epistemological, and logical significance of Buddhist doctrine, and religious scholars on the other side who devote their attention solely to religious praxis. Most scholars will agree, however, that, in Buddhism (and perhaps in all Asian traditions, for that matter) there is no clear-cut distinction between philosophy and religion, and that our tendency to favor one approach over another reflects the rigid boundaries within our own academic disciplines rather than anything inherent in the Buddhist tradition.

An approach to Buddhism that goes beyond this disciplinary split is obviously needed, and is what makes the doctrine of *upāya* both important and timely. It brings together the philosophical and religious by exploring the practices, meditation techniques, and religious disciplines in Buddhism, and offers a critical, philosophical analysis of Buddhist soteriology.

To understand what is at stake in this project it is important to distinguish between two types of philosophical reflection. In "Philosophy as Metapraxis," Thomas Kasulis describes a form of reflection devoted exclusively to problems surrounding the nature and efficacy of religious praxis (Kasulis 1992). He calls this "metapraxis," and argues that we need to distinguish it from other types of philosophical reflection—such as metaphysics—that problematize what stands behind or above religious praxis. Whereas metaphysical reflection is geared toward very general issues surrounding the nature of being, language, consciousness, and truth, metapractical reflection is geared specifically toward the efficacy of religious praxis: how beneficial it is, how it works, and whether it is performing its job adequately:

> Religious praxis generally has either a participatory or transformative function. It participates in, to use Rudolf Otto's term, the "numinous." It is transformative in its improving the person or community in some spiritual way (purifying, healing, reconciling, protecting, informing, and so on). Metapractical reflection inquires into the purpose and efficacy of the practice in terms of these participatory and transformative functions. Something happens, or at least is supposed to happen, in and through religious praxis. Metapraxis analyzes and evaluates that happening. What does the praxis change? Is something remembered? Reenacted? Empowered? If so, exactly how does the praxis work? And why should we prefer our traditional praxis as more effective than another? (Kasulis 1992, p. 178).

Kasulis' discussion of metapraxis will help us understand the significance of *upāya* and how it relates to Buddhism. The doctrine of *upāya* was developed by the Mahāyāna Buddhists to oppose the creation of an orthopraxy and to resist the tendency to confine the practices into an absolute path, or *mārga*. Early Mahāyāna texts such as the *Prajñāpāramitā*, *Lotus Sūtra*, and *Vimalakīrtinirdeśa* state that the Buddhist teachings are devised with a particular goal in mind and not abstract formulas to be espoused independently of knowing the exact dispositions of those who suffer. These early texts depict Śākyamuni as a "Great Physician" who knows the different types of illnesses of sentient beings and who can therefore offer the best "medicine" to suit their needs: he knows when to hold back, when to remain silent, and when to prescribe the appropriate antidote. To preach Buddhism without such sensitivity, we are often told, is "bad medicine."

Because *upāya* refers to a debate about the purpose and efficacy of Buddhist practice, it is not concerned with the nature of truth, consciousness, causality, or the self, and has no interest in solving pressing metaphysical dilemmas. It is thus different from the way most Western philosophers conceive of Buddhism. According to many scholars (Murti 1955, Conze 1973, Suzuki 1956, Robinson 1967, and Stcherbatsky 1968), Buddhist liberation has to do with releasing ourselves from the grip of grammatical fabrications, from logic, metaphysics, reason, conceptual dualities, and essentialism, and their texts are generally devoted to showing us how Buddhism deconstructs a fallacious view of personal identity, consciousness, and language.

"Skillful means" will counteract this "metaphysical" approach by arguing that the major debates in Buddhism surround issues of praxis and the problem of justifying a fixed practice for all people. This will be developed in a loosely chronological fashion, beginning with the historical Buddha in Chapter 1, which sets up the practice of "skill-in-means" through an analysis of the different pedagogical and heuristic devices outlined in the early Pāli texts, and is followed in Chapter 2 by an overview of the Abhidharma tradition in Buddhism. This chapter outlines the different metapractical theories of two important Abhidharma schools, which is essential to understanding why the doctrine of *upāya* was developed in the first place. The remaining three chapters offer different examples of "skill-in-means" in Buddhism. Chapter 3 explores the *Vimalakīrtinirdeśa*, an early

Mahāyāna text that condemns the Buddha's disciples for preaching "bad medicine." Chapter 4 focuses on the important Mahāyāna philosopher Nāgārjuna, and Chapter 5 discusses the role of *upāya* in the Ch'an and Pure Land traditions. The final section will conclude with some self-critical remarks regarding the upayic status of this entire study.

Hopefully, the reader will not walk away from this book with the feeling that Buddhism is simply relativistic, or with the sense that *upāya* restricts the study of Buddhism to mere historical analysis. On the contrary, it is hoped that the reader will glimpse the perennial value of *upāya* and its relevance to contemporary life and experience. For, while it is true that *upāya* speaks primarily to Buddhists about their own practices and about how not to become attached to Buddhism, it is fundamentally a teaching of compassion. It seeks to express love and intimacy, and shows how compassion is still possible in a world filled with confusion, unbearable suffering, and loneliness. It is this sense of compassion (*karuṇā*) that any book on *upāya* should try to convey.

Chapter 1

The Buddha's Skill-in-Means

Introduction

All Buddhists would agree that the most important event in Gautama Buddha's life was his enlightenment experience. As he sat meditating under the Bodhi Tree throughout the night, the Buddha experienced the depth of human suffering (*duḥkha*) and saw that bondage arises from the cyclical nature of attachments and desires. Later that same night, he perceived the law of "dependent co-origination" (*pratītya-samutpāda*) and felt that if one could break the cycle at the right point then one could achieve liberation. Just as dawn arrived, he cried, "Birth-and-death are finished! I have fulfilled my cherished goal!"

It is tempting to think that what the Buddha taught after his enlightenment was the "truth" of that experience, and that his goal as a teacher was to help others arrive at the same conclusion. It is also tempting to think that if enlightenment consists in discovering certain truths about the world then we will be enlightened if we can simply discover them as well. If we do think this way then we will easily neglect the rhetorical context of the Buddha's teachings and focus more on *what* he taught rather than *how* he taught. In the Mahāyāna Buddhist tradition, however, the Buddha's wisdom (*prajñā*) is not contained in a series of propositions or declarative statements about the world, but is expressed through a unique style of teaching, communicating, and responding to others. There is something about the way the

Buddha teaches that interests the Mahāyāna tradition, something about the way he speaks and the way he listens that reveals the depth of his enlightenment. By simply twirling a flower, touching someone on the shoulder, smiling, or gesturing with his finger he liberates sentient beings. For some, he simply offers words of advice and consolation, for others he gives long philosophical discourses on the nature of reality, and for others still, harsh reprimands. But what interests the early Mahāyānists is that all these forms of communication are effective: they all lead to enlightenment even though they differ in so many ways.

This interest in the Buddha's style of teaching needs to be distinguished from an abstract analysis of what the Buddha taught. Western philosophers who study Buddhism tend to examine the content of the Buddha's discourses at the expense of his pedagogical style, and assume that we can fully understand his message apart from its rhetorical context. Many think we can separate what the Buddha said from how he said it and to whom. For the early Mahāyānists, however, we will destroy the significance of the Buddha's teachings if we proceed in this way. Rather than searching for a "truth" behind his everyday use of words, the early Mahāyānists tell us that in order to fully appreciate the Buddha's philosophy we need to listen to how he communicates, how he teaches, and how he responds to others.

An example of this approach is the "Fire Sermon," which was given to a group of ascetic fire-worshippers who ritually burnt their own flesh. Because these devotees of *Agni* (the god of fire) engage in extreme self-mortification, the Buddha's way of communicating is to the point:

> All things, O priests, are on fire. And what, O priests, are these things which are on fire?

> The eye, O priests, is on fire; forms are on fire; eye-consciousness is on fire; impressions received by the eye are on fire; and whatever sensation, pleasant, unpleasant, or indifferent, originates in dependence on impression received by the eye, that also is on fire. And with what are these on fire? With the fire of passion, say I, with the fire of hatred, with the fire of infatuation; with birth, old age, death, sorrow, lamentation, misery, grief, and despair are they on fire. The ear is on fire...the tongue is on fire; tastes are on fire . . . the body is on fire; things tangible are on fire . . . the mind is on fire; ideas are on fire . . . mind-consciousness is on fire; impressions received by the mind are on fire; and whatever sensation, pleasant, unpleasant, or indifferent, originates in dependence on impressions received by the mind, that also is on fire. (Warren 1986, p. 236–239)

One could read this passage metaphysically, as saying something either about the nature of the world (that it is full of misery and hell-like) or about the nature of perception (that as long as there is "contact" between a sense organ and its object, there will be pain, unpleasantness, and grief). However, to read the "Fire Sermon" in this way would lead us to speculate on what the Buddha is saying in the abstract and apart from the fire worshipping priests who ritually burnt their own flesh. It would also lead us to ponder the metaphysical significance of his words apart from how they were communicated. Given the Buddha's desire to help these priests, however, he refuses to speak in the abstract. Instead, he uses words such as "fire" that directly appeal to their sensibilities and spiritual practices. If we neglect this rhetorical context then we will lose the soteriological force of this teaching that, we are told, convinced the chief fire-worshipper Uruvela Kasapa and his thousand followers to stop burning their bodies.

Another example is the Buddha's "First Sermon at Banaras" given to the five ascetics the Buddha once lived with in the mountains. As with the fire-worshipping priests, the Buddha considers their practices harmful and self-destructive, and he tries to catch their attention by using words that appeal to their own world-view:

> How is there laughter, how is there joy, as this world is always burning? Do you not seek a light, you who are surrounded by darkness?
> Look at this dressed-up lump, covered with wounds, joined together sickly, full of many schemes, but which has no strength, no hold!
> This body is wasted, full of sickness, and frail; this heap of corruption breaks to pieces, life indeed ends in death. (Warren 1986, p. 236–239)

The universality of *duḥkha* (suffering) is expressed in the Buddha's "First Sermon," and is considered one of the "three marks" (*lakṣaṇa*) of existence. If we read the sermon in its rhetorical context, however, it is doubtful we will derive a metaphysical conclusion. As in the "Fire Sermon," the Buddha is not referring to misery (*duḥkha*) as an abstract category. He is speaking to ascetics who already have a pessimistic view of life, and he agrees with them. In fact, he emphasizes just how miserable and sick life really is. After getting their attention, he tells them that their extreme way of life only causes more self-injury and pain, and that it is not possible to achieve liberation through such extreme measures: "The emaciated devotee produces confusion and sickly thoughts in his mind. Mortification is not conducive even to worldly knowledge." The Buddha then teaches them the "Middle Way," which avoids the extremes of self-mortification and indulgence. If the Buddha had spoken metaphysically or ignored their emotional and intellectual context, it is doubtful the ascetics would have ever listened.

The point about keeping the rhetorical context of the Buddha's teachings in mind is that it draws our attention to how compassion is expressed through the teachings. A common weakness in a metaphysical reading is that it privileges what the Buddha said over how he said it, and gives the impression that he spoke with no particular person in mind. This not only effaces the Buddha's own style of religious praxis—his manner of teaching and responding to others—but, from a skillful means perspective, kills what is most distinctive about the Buddha's teachings: his compassion.

Skillful Teachings

Given the Buddha's realization that he needs to respond to the world in different ways, a number of Mahāyāna texts say the Buddha teaches a variety of philosophical and religious views that suit the contextual dispositions of his audience. The *Lotus Sūtra* says:

> Did I not say before that the buddhas, the world-honored ones, proclaim the Dharma by various karmic reasonings, parables, forms of words and skillful means, all for the sake of supreme, perfect enlightenment? (Kern 1989, p. 103)

The famous Mādhyamika philosopher Nāgārjuna repeats this view when he says:

> The teachings of the protectors of the world accord with the [varying] resolve of living beings. The Buddhas employ a wealth of skillful means, which take many worldly forms. (Lindtner 1986, p. 65)

Even the idea of *nirvāṇa*, according to many Mahāyāna texts, is simply another "skillful means" of the Buddha:

> For this reason, Śāriputra,
> I set up a skillful means for them,
> Expounding the way to end all sufferings,
> And showing it by nirvāṇa. (Kern 1989, p. 54)

The Mahāyāna sūtras are full of stories that express the Buddha's compassionate activities, some of which even go against orthodox Buddhist doctrine. The *Upāyakauśalya Sūtra* tells of a young woman who was so in love with the Buddha that she was prepared to kill herself if the Buddha refused her. Out of compassion, the Buddha broke his vow of celibacy and had a sexual affair with the woman (Tatz 1994, p. 34). Another story from the same text tells how the Buddha in a former life actually murdered a man. His reason was to prevent the man from killing 500 others, and the only way to prevent this was to kill him. The Buddha's act was motivated solely from compassion—both for those who were about to be murdered as well as for the murderer—and the Buddha went against his own moral principles and was willing to suffer in hell because of it. (Tatz 1994, p. 73–77)

The most significant feature of *upāya* is that liberation does not stem from a metaphysical vision of humanity or a "mystical" union with truth. The *Lotus Sūtra* tells the story of a rich man who lures his children out of a burning house by promising them beautiful gifts (Kern 1989, p. 94). Traditionally, the house represents the realm of delusion and ignorance, the "imaginary" gifts are the Buddha's teaching styles, and the "bare ground" outside the house represents the realm of enlightenment. The moral of the story is that enlightenment does not depend on any particular metaphysical view since the children are liberated though an imaginary "device."

What is puzzling about such stories is that they not only go against orthodox Buddhist doctrine—they seem philosophically inconsistent. That the Buddha can kill, lie, or cheat to help others attain liberation, and that he can say different things to different people—and yet still achieve the same end—seems like sophistry. A good example of this problem is found in the *Brahma Vihāra* where the Buddha instructs two young brahmins on how to attain union with the Hindu god Brahmā. The puzzling aspect of this story is that we not only find the Buddha teaching ideas that seem more Hindu than Buddhist, but that he seems to contradict the doctrine of "non-self" (*anātman*), which many scholars see as the Buddha's real philosophical position. According to this doctrine, all things are "selfless" and non-substantial, and the entire universe lacks an underlying force or metaphysical being, like Brahmā. Nevertheless, when the Buddha encounters two young brahmins who are confused about their own Hindu teachings, he instructs them in the following way:

> And he lets his mind pervade one quarter of the world with thoughts of love, and so the second, and so the third, and so forth. And thus the whole wide world,

> above, below, around and everywhere, does he continue to pervade with heart of love, far reaching, grown great, and beyond measure. Just as a mighty trumpeter makes himself heard—and that without difficulty—in all the four directions; even so of all things that have shape or life, there is not one that he passes by or leaves aside, but regards them all with mind set free, and deep felt love. Verily this . . . is the way to a state of union with Brahma. (*Brahma Vihāra*, trans. by Rhys-Davids 1899, p. 310)

Rather than telling the brahmins that there is no "self," no God, no Brahmā, and no metaphysical basis to life, he offers them advice on the best way to attain union with a god.

Such inconsistencies are found throughout the Pāli discourses. In the following section from the *Saṃyutta-Nikāya*, for example, the Buddha tells his disciples that they should not search for anything transcendental or beyond sense experience:

> Monks, I will teach you "everything." Listen to it. What, monks, is "everything"? Eye and material form, ear and sound, nose and odor, tongue and taste, body and tangible objects, mind and mental objects. These are called "everything." Monks, he who would say: "I reject this everything and proclaim another everything," he may certainly have a theory [of his own]. But when questioned, he would not be able to answer and would, moreover, be subject to vexation. Why? Because it would not be within the range of sense-experience. (*Saṃyutta-Nikāya*, quoted in Kalupahana 1976, p. 158)

But in other passages the Buddha seems to describe ultimate reality as transcendental and beyond the senses:

> The stopping of becoming is Nirvāṇa. (*Saṃyutta-Nikāya* II, 117)

> Nirvāṇa do I call it—the utter extinction of aging and dying. (*Saṃyutta-Nikāya* I, 39)

> There is, monks, that plane where there is neither extension nor . . . motion nor the plane of infinite ether . . . nor that of neither-perception-nor-non-perception, neither this world nor another, neither the moon nor the sun. Here, monks, I say that there is no coming or going or remaining or deceasing or uprising, for this is itself without support, without continuance, without mental object—this is itself the end of suffering. There is, monks, an unborn, not become, not made, uncompounded, and were it not, monks, for this unborn, not become, not made, uncompounded, no escape could be shown here for what is born, has become, is made, is compounded. But because there is, monks, an unborn, not become, not made, uncompounded, therefore an escape can be shown for what is born, has become, is made, is compounded. (*Udāna* 80–81)

How should we understand these obvious inconsistencies in the Buddha's teachings? The Mahāyāna tradition struggled with this and came up with various ways to resolve it. One way was to say the Buddha never intended all of his teachings to be taken literally. Texts like the *Saṃdhinirmocana Sūtra* say the Buddha spoke some doctrines "conventionally" and others "ultimately"—meaning that some of his sayings were merely for the ignorant while others were withheld for the more advanced—while other texts like the *Lotus Sūtra* make no distinction between the skillful and non-skillful teaching: "Apart from the skillful means of the Buddha," says the *Lotus Sūtra*, "there is no other vehicle to be found."

From a traditional Western philosophical stance, the skillful means approach makes the Buddha either logically incompetent or a sophist who is more interested in playing games with people than telling the truth. The philosopher Richard Garner takes this approach and wonders why the Buddha lies to people. He sees this as a major flaw in the Buddha's philosophy, and says it would have been better had he simply spoken the truth (Garner, 1993). However, to frame the issue of *upāya* in terms of "truth" may be misleading here. That the Buddha may have "lied" or taught incompatible positions is, from a purely logical perspective, a sign of poor judgement or irrational thinking. But from a skillful means perspective it expresses an ability to respond to the various forms of suffering the Buddha encountered on a daily basis. The point of all those stories in which the Buddha supposedly lies or contradicts himself is not to condone those activities, any more than a story about the Buddha killing someone is meant to justify murder. Rather, the point is to show that suffering is a deeply personal experience that is irreducible to an abstract category or general rule. No two people suffer in the same way, and when the Buddha changes his "view" he is simply responding to the unique karmic formations of human beings. This does not mean, as Peter Hershock says:

> [That] there is a level of generality where we can speak and reason intelligibly about suffering . . . . What is be-

> ing denied is that whatever is so discussed has ever been actually experienced by any living creature and that such discussions have any real bearing on resolving the always unique sufferings and hungers by which sentient beings are often bound. (Hershock 1996, p. 9)

Thus, the issue in the Buddha's supposed "inconsistencies" is not about truth in the abstract but about how to respond to the concrete manifestations of *duḥkha*. From the perspective of "skillful means," his ability to shift viewpoints shows that wisdom (*prajñā*) is not bound by any single doctrine, practice, or metaphysical view, and exhibits the transformative intimacy of a Bodhisattva's love.

Did the Buddha Have a Philosophical Position?

While skillful means draws our attention to the pedagogical style of the Buddha, Buddhist scholars in the West still disagree over the Buddha's real philosophical position. Does he offer a coherent and systematic view of the world? Does he teach any metaphysical doctrines he thinks are true? Does he think that final liberation depends on knowing something about the nature of reality? To answer these questions we should examine an important passage from the *Brahmajāla-suttanta* in which the Buddha responds to "sixty-two" philosophical views (*dṛṣṭi)* that prevailed in India during his time. "In this way and that," says the Buddha referring to the proponents of these "sixty-two" views:

> they plunge about in the net of these sixty-two modes, but they are in it; this way and that they flounder, but

they are included in it, caught in it. (*Brahmajāla-suttanta,* trans. by Rhys-Davids 1899, p. 54)

The "net" these views share is a form of "extremism" the Buddha considers harmful, and he reduces them to one of two positions: existence or non-existence. The Brahmanic, Sāṅkhya, and Jain traditions exemplify the extreme of "existence" since they ground their views in an eternal substance, be it *Brahman*, *Puruṣa*, or the *jīvas*, and the Cārvāka tradition is an example of "non-existence" since it reduces all experience to material substances. Even though each tradition has radically different views on the nature of life, they also share a form of "extremism" which the Buddha saw as a major source of suffering and conflict in life. Dissatisfied with each of the "sixty-two" philosophical views, he forged a different path: "Without approaching either extreme, the Tathāgata teaches you the Doctrine of the Middle."

What does the Buddha mean by calling these views extreme, and what is the "Doctrine of the Middle"? To answer this we need to remember that the Buddha is trying to solve a crisis among the Indian philosophical traditions. The Brahmanic, Jain, Cārvāka, and other ascetic traditions are all engaged in an intellectual and spiritual battle, and the Buddha is trying to resolve their differences by pointing to the source of their conflict. What is it that all these "sixty-two" views share?

A number of Western scholars see the conflict between the "sixty-two" views as a metaphysical problem. That is, they see the problem arising because each of the views has an incoherent view of the world. According to T. R. V. Murti, for example, the problem lies in the fact that all these various traditions are trying to conceptualize the nature of reality, and the Buddha's way of resolving the issue is to reject all forms of conceptualization:

> The rejection of theories [*dṛṣṭi*] is itself the *means* by which Buddha is led to the non-conceptual knowledge of the absolute, and not vice versa. It is no accident then that Buddha concerns himself with an analysis of the various theories of reality and rejects them all. Buddha ascends from the conflict of Reason to the inexpressibility of the absolute. (Murti 1955, p. 47)

Murti sees the problem between the "sixty-two" views as a metaphysical problem: they all have incorrect views of the world and think that ultimate reality can be rationally and conceptually explained. Because the conflict for Murti is rooted in conceptualization, he sees the Buddha resolving it by rejecting *all* philosophical (i.e., conceptual) positions. Gadjin Nagao echoes this sentiment when he says, "Ultimate Truth is beyond the reach of verbal designation (*prapañca*) or thought-construct (*vikalpa*)" (Nagao 1991, p. 40), as does David Loy who sees the Buddha deconstructing false views of language and conceptualization (Loy 1987).

David Kalupahana sees the conflict between the "sixty-two" views differently. In his view, the problem with the "sixty-two" views is that they all go beyond empirical verification. What makes the "sixty-two" false is not that they utilize words and concepts, as Murti and others think, but that they fail to confine themselves "to what is given, that is, to the causal dependence of phenomena, without searching for something mysterious" (Kalupahana 1986, p. 13). Because Kalupahana sees the conflict between the "sixty-two" stemming from a desire for something non-empirical, he sees the Buddha rejecting all forms of transcendentalism and teaching a "sixty-third" view: the doctrine of "dependent arising," which, as he says, is empirically verifiable: "It is, indeed, the truth about the world which the Buddha claimed he discovered and which became the 'central' doctrine of Buddhism" (Kalupahana 1976, p. 29).

Although Kalupahana sees the issue in a different light, he shares with Murti, Loy, and Nagao the belief that the Buddha is engaged in a metaphysical battle with the "sixty-two" views. That is, they all see the conflict between the "sixty-two" views as being caused by false metaphysics, and they all see the Buddha resolving the conflict by showing what is really "true."

However, these ways of resolving the problem are questionable because they all assume that the philosophical traditions are fighting *because* they have false metaphysical views. According to Buddhism, however, "views" (*dṛṣṭis*) in themselves do not cause conflicts. Rather, it is our *attachments* to "views" that causes so many problems in life. By itself, a "view" is relatively innocuous, and there is nothing inconsistent in adhering to any number of "false" or "extreme" views without engaging in any conflicts. It is what lies *behind* our "views" that is the real issue for Buddhists. According to the "Second Noble Truth," suffering, conflict, and strife (*duḥkha*) are caused by "blind grasping" and attachment. This attachment causes suffering and conflict in the world, and not, as some scholars think, by simply having a false view of the world. Even the idea that "things" have permanence, a heresy in many Buddhist quarters, is not inherently tainted or incorrect so long as we are unattached to it. In the following dialogue between the Buddha and a brahmin, for example, the Buddha expresses his real problem with certain philosophical positions:

> "Venerable Gautama, there are the ancient holy scriptures of the Brahmins handed down along the line by unbroken oral tradition of texts. With regard to them, Brahmins come to the absolute conclusion: 'This alone is Truth, and everything else is false.' Now, what does the Venerable Gautama say about this?"
>
> The Buddha inquired: "Among Brahmins is there any one single Brahmin who claims that he personally knows and sees that 'This alone is Truth, and everything else is false'?"
>
> "No."
>
> "Then, is there any one single teacher, or a teacher of teachers of Brahmins back to the seventh generation, or even any of the original authors of those scriptures, who claims that he knows and he sees: 'This alone is Truth, and everything else is false'?"
>
> "No."
>
> "Then, it is like a line of blind men, each holding on to the preceding one; the first one does not see, the middle one also does not see, the last one also does not see. Thus, it seems to me that the state of the Brahmins is like that of a line of blind men." (*Majjhima-Nikāya*, quoted in Rahula 1974, p. 10)

Then the Buddha gave his advice: "It is not proper for a wise man who maintains truth to come to the conclusion: 'This alone is Truth, and everything else is false.' . . . A man has a faith. If he says, 'This is my faith,' so far he maintains truth. But by that he cannot proceed to the absolute conclusion: 'This alone is Truth and everything else is false.'"

The Buddha's problem with these brahmins has little to do with their metaphysical presuppositions. In fact, it appears he could care less whether their views are transcendental, nihilistic, atheistic, or empirical. Rather than attacking their philosophical assumptions, he questions their attachments. Why are they so attached to their own views, and why do they think their own views are the only acceptable ones? In asking this, the Buddha is addressing what lies *behind* their views rather than the views themselves.

It is important to remember that the "sixty-two" views are all paths to liberation (*mārgas*). They are all trying to liberate human beings in their own way, and they offer various meditation techniques and religious disciplines to achieve this end. The problem for the Buddha is that the people who espouse these "views" are attached to them, and therefore assume that there is only one path to liberation. While they think they are helping others, they actually cause more suffering and strife in the world.

The Buddha's own position is different. Rather than proposing another "view" over and above the "sixty two," he teaches non-attachment to any particular view or spiritual praxis. In a famous section from the *Majjhima-Nikāya* called "Crossing over by Raft," for example, the Buddha clearly states that his teachings should not become objects of attachment.

> Monks, I will teach you Dhamma—the Parable of the Raft—for crossing over, not for retaining. Listen to it, attend carefully, and I will speak. A man going along a high-road might see a great stretch of water, the hither

> bank frightening. But if there were no boat for crossing by or a bridge across for going from the not-beyond to the beyond, he might think: 'If I were to collect sticks, grass, branches foliage and to tie a raft, then, depending on the raft and striving with my hands and feet, I might cross over safely to the beyond.' If he carried out his purpose, then, crossed over, gone beyond, it might occur to him: 'Now, this raft has been very useful to me. Depending on it and striving with my hands and feet, I have crossed over safely to the beyond. Suppose now, having put this raft on my head or lifted it on to my shoulder, I should proceed as I desire?' Now, monks, in doing this is that man doing what should be done with that raft? (Conze 1954, p. 87–88)

As the Buddha explains in this passage, the Dharma is a "raft," and since the Dharma includes the ideas of *nirvāṇa*, dependent arising, non-self (*anātman*), impermanence, and "emptiness," they too are nothing more than provisional devices used to help others. As "rafts," it would be absurd to think of them in propositional terms, or as applying to all situations and contexts. This would be to accept the Dharma as more than a "raft," as something we should carry around after reaching the other "shore." The Buddha makes a similar remark regarding "dependent arising":

> O, Bhikkus, even this view, which is so pure and so clear, if you cling to it, if you fondle it, if you treasure it, if you are attached to it, then you do not understand that the teaching is similar to a raft, which is for crossing over, and not for getting hold of. (Rahula 1974, p. 11)

The teaching of "dependent arising" is central to all Buddhist traditions, and yet the Buddha warns against becoming attached to it. To "fondle" *pratītya-samutpāda*, to treasure it, is to treat it in a non-*upāyic* way—as something more than a provisional "raft" used to help others. This may lead one to say, "This alone is truth, and everything else is false."

The Western philosopher Ludwig Wittgenstein makes a similar point regarding his own teachings:

> My propositions serve as elucidations in the following way: anyone who understands me eventually recognizes them as nonsensical, when he has used them—as steps—to climb up beyond them. (He must, so to speak, throw away the ladder after he has climbed up it.) (Wittgenstein 1953, p. 74)

While the Buddha would not subscribe to much of what Wittgenstein says in the *Tractatus*, the metaphor of an abandoned ladder fits the Buddha's teachings well. One should not become attached to the teachings since they are, ultimately, teachings of non-attachment.

The Buddha's view of non-attachment is also similar to William James' philosophy, which bracketed questions concerning the "truth value" of religious statements. In *The Varieties of Religious Experience*, James explores the various ways in which people are transformed through religious experiences, and says, "Not by its origin, but *the way in which it works on the whole*," expressing his unwillingness to judge a religious experience apart from how it "works" as a lived event (James 1936, p. 21). James' depiction of the "sick soul" versus the "healthy-minded" soul shows how the same metaphysical or religious view can impact people's lives in fundamentally different ways. Whereas an experience of God can make one person emotionally dark and depressed, for another it can inspire peace and tranquillity. Pye remarks on a similar idea when he says that, according to Buddhism, "the same item of doctrine may be both a barrier and a door depending on how it is used" (Pye 1978, p. 134). The Buddha would agree with James' approach in that it refuses to reduce the truth of a religious experience to mere factual coherence or "meaningful statements." The value of any particular philosophical or religious view lies in its effectiveness that cannot be determined apart from the way it plays itself out in people's lives.

Following James' approach to religion, we should now see why a metaphysical understanding of Buddhism falls short. It not only assumes that the problems of existence are caused by incorrect views of the world, but that liberation entails the recognition of what is really real. This approach privileges theory over praxis, and metaphysics over ethics, and assumes that a Buddhist response to the world—to other human beings and their real embodied suffering—means going beyond their concrete differences to an underlying, single cause. In this way, we lose sight of an entire history of Buddhism that has always privileged religious praxis, discipline, and spiritual methodology over abstract theory and speculation. As Robert Buswell says:

> [The] Buddha is said to have identified himself as "analyzer" rather than as a "dogmatist" or someone who makes categorical assertions. This reasoning seems also to justify the characteristically Buddhist invocation of pragmatic criteria for the evaluation of doctrines and

> practices . . . . It is not unexpected, therefore, that Buddhists should regularly choose disciplined experience (e.g., meditation) over reason, revelation, and authority as the final arbiter of religious truth or efficacy. (Buswell 1992, p. 4)

When we think of the Buddha's critique of the "sixty-two" views in the context of skillful means, we do not see him asking *what* the world is like but how to achieve liberation and how to be compassionate. The philosophical problem in this approach rests on how one negotiates this soteriological terrain. Which methodology should I use? What is the best way to overcome suffering and help others? How do I achieve liberation and help others do so as well? The "sixty-two" views answer these questions by offering different spiritual practices and meditation techniques to achieve this end, but each one assumes there is only one methodological path for everyone—their own. The Buddha rejects this as dogmatic, and says that we should refrain from being attached to any single teaching, discipline, or religious method, including his own.

The Buddha's Noble Silence

We are now in a position to appreciate one of the most puzzling issues in early Buddhism: the Buddha's "Noble Silence." His response to what is traditionally called the "fourteen unanswered questions," or *avyākṛta,* is by no means easy to decipher, especially since silence can be interpreted in any number of ways. Nevertheless, if we keep in mind the Buddha's desire to help others overcome attachment and suffering, then his reason for remaining silent should become clear.

The most famous example of the "unanswered questions" occurs in the *Majjhima-Nikāya* where a disciple of the Buddha, Malunkyaputta, demands to know why the Buddha refuses to answer certain questions:

> Thus have I heard. On a certain occasion The Blessed One was dwelling at Sarvatthi in Jetavana monastery in Anathapindika's Park. Now it happened to the venerable Malunkyaputta, being in seclusion and plunged in meditation, that a consideration presented itself to his mind as follows: "These theories which the Blessed One has left unelucidated, has set aside and rejected—that the world is eternal, that the world is not eternal, that the world is finite, that the world is infinite, that the soul and the body are identical, that the soul is one thing and the body another, that the saint exists after death, that the saint does not exist after death, that the saint both exists and does not exist after death, that the saint neither exists nor does not exist after death,—these The Blessed One does not elucidate to me. And the fact the Blessed One does not elucidate them to me does not please me nor suit me. Therefore I will draw near to The Blessed One and inquire of him concerning this matter. (*Majjhima-Nikāya*, trans. by Warren 1986, p. 117)

Malunkyaputta then goes to the Buddha and adds that if he fails to solve these problems then he will not practice Buddhism and will return to a regular life. By joining the pairs, eternal-non-eternal and infinite-finite, there are fourteen questions the Buddha refused to answer:

1. Is the Universe eternal?
2. Is the Universe non-eternal?
3. Is the Universe at one and the same time eternal and non-eternal?
4. Is the universe neither eternal nor non-eternal?
5. Is the universe infinite?
6. Is the universe finite?
7. Is the universe at one and the same time infinite and finite?
8. Is the universe neither infinite nor finite?
9. Is the soul identical to the body?
10. Is the soul different from the body?
11. Does the Tathāgata survive death?
12. Does the Tathāgata not survive death?
13. Does the Tathāgata both survive death and not survive death?
14. Does the Tathāgata neither survive death nor not survive death?

The above questions refer in one way or another back to the "sixty-two" views the Buddha refused to accept. The first eight refer to the extent and duration of the world, the next two to the nature of personal identity, and the last four to the status of the dead saint, or, more specifically, to life after death. We have already seen that the Buddha dismissed all of the "sixty-two" views because each dogmatically asserts, "This alone is Truth, and everything else is false." In regards to the specific questions listed above, however, the Buddha was unwilling to offer any positive critique whatsoever, which has puzzled Buddhist scholars for centuries. Before we examine some Western solutions to this puzzle, it might be helpful to listen to what the Buddha has to say regarding his silence. After Malunkyaputta asks the Buddha why he refuses to answer the questions, the Buddha responds with the following remark:

> The religious life, Malunkyaputta, does not depend on the view that the world is eternal; nor does the religious life, Malunkyaputta, depend on the dogma that the world is not eternal. Whether the view obtains, Malunkyaputta, that the world is eternal, or that the world is not eternal, there still remain birth, old age, death, sorrow, lamentation, misery, grief, and despair.... Why Malunkyaputta, have I not explained this? Because, Malunkyaputta, this profits not, nor has to do with the fundamentals of religion, nor tends to aversion, absence of passion, cessation, quiescence, supreme wisdom, and Nirvāṇa; therefore, have I not explained it? (Warren 1986, p. 119)

The Buddha also tells Malunkyaputta that his demand for an answer is like a man who has been shot by a poison arrow, but who demands to know who shot the arrow, what it is made of, what tree it came from, and so on, all before the arrow is pulled (Warren 1986, p. 122). In other words, the Buddha chides Malunkyaputta for demanding answers to questions that have nothing to do with his ability to overcome hatred, greed, and blind attachment. Because the Buddha knows Malunkyaputta's past as a Hindu practitioner, and because he knows that Malunkyaputta will not be satisfied due to his desperation to have an answer, the Buddha refuses to respond, knowing that any answer will only cause more suffering on Malunkyaputta's part. The issue for the Buddha is not whether the questions *can* be answered, or whether they reflect propositionally true or false statements regarding existence, but whether these questions are soteriologically relevant for Malunkyaputta. He therefore advises Malunkyaputta not to worry about questions regarding the origin of the universe, the soul, or life after death, and tells him that his silence regarding such questions is itself the answer: "Therefore, have I not explained it?" meaning that such questions are irrelevant to his own situation and context.

This skillful means approach to the Buddha's silence is found in another story where the Buddha refused to answer questions that on other occasions he did answer. The story occurs when a certain wandering monk named Vacchagotta asks the Buddha whether there is an *ātman*:

> "Venerable Gautama, is there an *ātman*?"
> The Buddha is silent.
> "Then Venerable Gautama, is there no *ātman*?"
> Again the Buddha is silent.
> Vacchagotta gets up and goes away.
> After the Parivrajaka (Wanderer) had left, Ānanda asks the Buddha why he did not answer Vacchagota's question. The Buddha explains his position:
> "Ānanda, when asked by Vacchagotta the Wanderer: 'Is there a self?', if I had answered: 'there is a self,' then, Ānanda, that would be siding with those recluses and brahmins who hold the eternalist theory.
> "And, Ānanda, when asked by the Wanderer: 'Is there no self?', if I had answered: 'There is no self,' then

that would be siding with those recluses and brahmins who hold the annihilationist theory.

"Again, Ānanda, when asked by Vacchagotta: 'Is there a self?', if I had answered: 'There is a self,' would that be in accordance with my knowledge that all *dhammas* are without self?"

"Surely not, Sir."

"And again, Ānanda, when asked by the Wanderer: 'Is there no self?', if I had answered: 'There is no self,' then that would have been a greater confusion to the already confused Vacchagotta. For he would have thought: Formerly indeed I had a self, but now I haven't got one." (Quoted in Rahula 1974, p. 62–63)

In this story, the Buddha explains why he remains silent: it has to do with the specific needs and problems of a particular person. Whether he thinks there really is a "self" is irrelevant in this case since he is interested in helping Vacchagotta overcome his confusions. If the Buddha believed that truth is the best "medicine" and something to be spoken in every context, then he would have answered Vacchagotta. But he knew that any answer—even a true one—would make matters worse. Rahula comments on this story in the following way:

> There are many references in the Pāli texts to this same Vacchagotta the Wanderer, his going round quite often to see the Buddha and his disciples and putting the same kind of question again and again, evidently very much worried, almost obsessed by these problems. The Buddha's silence seems to have had much more effect

on Vacchagotta than any eloquent answer or discussion. (Rahula 1974, p. 64)

Most Western scholars think of the Buddha's silence as pointing to something more mysterious and metaphysically deep than a simple heuristic device. T. R. V. Murti says that the "true nature" of the Buddha's silence "can only be interpreted as meaning the consciousness of the indescribable nature of the Unconditioned Reality" (Murti 1955, p. 48); and Gadjin Nagao says that "the inadequacy of language must be regarded as an important key in understanding the problem of the fourteen unanswered questions," since, for the Buddha, "Ultimate Truth is beyond the reach of verbal designation or thought construct" (Nagao 1991, p. 40). For Murti and Nagao, as well as many other Buddhist writers, silence was the only legitimate response the Buddha could have offered since there is no other way to reveal what exists beyond language and concepts except by showing it through the gesture of a "noble silence."

Kalupahana opposes this "transcendental" reading of the Buddha's silence because a non-linguistic or non-conceptual experience is not empirically acceptable. For him, the Buddha's silence is an attempt to stop people from asking "metaphysical" questions:

> Since no answer based on experience is possible, the Buddha remained silent when pressed for an answer and maintained that the questions as to whether the *tathagata* exists (*hoti*) or arises (*uppajjati*), does not exist or does not arise, both or neither, do not fit the case (*na upeti*). It is like asking whether unicorns exist or not.... As the Logical Positivists themselves maintain,

> (such) metaphysical statements are meaningless because they are not verified in experience. (Kalupahana 1976, p. 157)

Troy Organ is one of the few Buddhist scholars to explicate the idea that the Buddha's response should be seen pragmatically:

> The picture we get of the Buddha is that of a remarkably single-minded man. Speculation was not only useless but harmful, for it would sidetrack him from his main goal. He had no disinterested love for truth. He admitted that he had more truths which he might disclose, but he refrained and limited himself to the revelation of only those truths which he considered to be religiously significant. Truth was a value for him only when it was a means to man's release from suffering. For Gautama, all knowledge was ideology, that is, all knowledge was held and expressed for certain reasons. His *dharma* was revealed only because it contributed to man's salvation. (Organ 1954, p. 130)

From a skillful means perspective, Organ's approach is more in accord with the Buddha's philosophy. In the two stories cited above, the Buddha states his reasons for remaining silent, and they have nothing to do with the idea that language is either a barrier to ultimate truth or a set of propositions that should be verified on empirical grounds. Instead, the Buddha tells Malunkyaputta that such questions "tend not to edification," in other words, that they are irrelevant to Malunkyaputta's own problem of overcoming attachment. Likewise, when he tells Ānanda why he refuses to answer

Vacchagotta's question about the existence of *ātman*, there is no evidence to suggest that what he *really* meant was that such questions are beyond the scope of language. He simply says that he does not want to confuse Vacchagotta any further. Rather than pointing to anything metaphysical, either the extra-linguistic or Logical Positivist type, the Buddha's silence appears more *upāyistic*, signifying nothing more than a simple desire to help others.

While it is certainly difficult to arrive at any definitive conclusion about the Buddha's Noble Silence, a metaphysical reading misses the mark because it severs the Buddha's silence from its rhetorical and pedagogical context where it was expressed as a compassionate response. To think of it as pointing to a deeper reality untouched by words or conceptual frameworks destroys the soteriological encounter in which silence is simply one of the various ways a Buddha responds to others.

Summary

This chapter introduced the idea that the Buddha's teachings are best understood as religious tools and methodological devices for helping others rather than metaphysical or epistemological truths. If we take the Buddha's initial hesitation to teach seriously, and if we accept his decision to teach only in relation to the contextual needs and dispositions of his audience, then it is a mistake to focus on the doctrinal aspects of the Buddha's teachings apart from how they were communicated. The Buddha's first sermons were given to his former companions, severe ascetics who were trying to discover the "Self" through self-mortification. It is thus no wonder why he tells them to avoid extremes by staying in the "middle," and even less confusing why he says there is no *ātman*. Both teachings make obvious sense when taking his audience and rhetorical context into account.

The following section will continue the theme of skillful means by looking at how the early Buddhists became attached to the Dharma. It was not long after the Buddha's death that a highly sectarian form of scholasticism developed in India, and Buddhists began debating among themselves over the status of the Buddha's teachings. There soon developed organized sects or schools, each with its own body of literature and philosophical texts known as the *abhidharma*. In itself, the *abdhidharma* provides a fascinating glimpse into early Buddhist meditation and practice in which every aspect of experience is microscopically analyzed and reflected upon. But the philosophers of these texts went further by trying to philosophically justify a normative view of praxis and saying that one had to meditate on the *abhidharma* in order to attain liberation.

The Mahāyāna tradition, which is the focus of Chapters 3 and 4, scolds the Abhidharma philosophers for becoming attached to the Dharma and for reducing Buddhism to an abstract system of rules and religious disciplines. Nāgārjuna even develops a sophisticated dialectical method to attack the Abhidharma. His philosophy of *śūnyatā*, or "emptiness," is a continuation of the Buddha's silence on a higher philosophical level: whereas the Buddha refused to answer certain questions, Nāgārjuna provides a whole series of *reductios* that attempt to uproot, through deconstructive logic, the desire to fixate on methodological views (*dṛṣṭis*) and religious practices. The whole process of his dialectic, as we will see, is a skillful means, and what Nāgārjuna calls "the emptiness of emptiness" is the embodiment of the Buddha's entire approach to philosophy as *upāya*.

Chapter 2

Abhidharma Buddhism: The Scholastic Tradition

Introduction

In some of the Buddha's most important teachings, he rejects the idea of an eternal, independent, or substantial "self," and develops the idea that a person is composed of a complex inter-relation between the five aggregates (*skandha*) such as form (*rūpa*), feelings (*vedanā*), perceptions (*saññā*), volitions (*saṁskāra*), and consciousness (*vijñāna*). Like Nāgasena's analysis of the chariot, the *skandha* theory implies that a person cannot be reduced to any single part, nor is it something different from all parts put together. Rather, a person is an interrelated whole, a dynamic interchange between the *skandhas* in which each part is necessary and in which no part can be extracted without losing the whole person.

The Buddha proposed the *skandhas* against the Hindu view of an eternal Self behind our daily experience, and against the *Cārvāka* view that rejects everything but our material existence. Arguing against both positions, the Buddha proposed a relational view of experience in which the concrete wholeness of a person is neither lost by searching for an unchanging self (eternalism) nor denied by reducing the self to its mere material parts (nihilism). In arguing for a relational view of *skandhas*, however, the Buddha warned against seeing them as static categories of experience: they too are "empty" (*śūnya*) and without substance (*anātman*), and therefore fully conditioned and inter-related aspects of experience. Thus, a person is not relational as a universal category but in the concrete: her experiences depend on where she is in life, how she interprets the world, and what her overall dispositional character is like.

The *abhidharma* literature is a significant step in this way of thinking due to its sophisticated disciplines that allow a person to explore the relational nature of experience. It provides step-by-step procedures for experiencing the world as inter-related and conditioned, and for losing a sense of "self" that clings to things as static and independent. The *abhidharma* texts analyze *skandhas* into finer experiential units (*dharmas*) and show how particular moments of pain, suffering, joy, lust, greed, anxiety, and so on are all dependently originated and conditioned, and how all experience is deeply intertwined within a vast causal nexus.

While the *abhidharma* literature offers us a glimpse into early Buddhist meditation and praxis, however, the later Abhidharma philosophers developed sophisticated metapractical arguments to justify the type of praxis embodied in the *abhidharma* texts. That is, they tried to philosophically justify the *abhidharma* as the "highest" form of Buddhist praxis (Kalupahana 1986; Jayatilleke 1963). The Sarvāstivāda and Sautrāntika schools, for example, elevated the *abhidharma* to the "literal" teachings of the Buddha, saying that it contained the "real" soteriological guidelines for everyone. Whether one wanted to attain liberation, help others overcome suffering, or live a compassionate life, one needed to meditate by following the particular steps outlined in the *abhidharma* texts.

As will be shown in Chapter 3, Mahāyāna Buddhism originated as an attack against this way of justifying the *abhidharma* texts. The development of "skillful means" is a critical weapon against what the Mahāyāna Buddhists see as attachment to Buddhist praxis: in privileging one set of texts and one type of meditation, the Abhidharma Buddhists have neglected the complexity of human development and reduced Buddhism to a static doctrine. The Dharma, however, must remain open, according to the Mahāyāna Buddhists, and is why they emphasize the "emptiness" of all the Buddha's teachings. Before we examine this Mahāyāna response to the Abhidharma tradition, a clear understanding of Abhidharma philosophy is necessary. The following sections of this chapter outline two important Abhidharma schools, the Sarvāstivāda and Sautrāntika, paying special attention to the issue of causality that is central to this tradition as a whole.

Early Buddhist Schisms

The previous chapter noted the Buddha's warning to not reduce all religious practice to a fixed mold. His disciples were never fully content with this, however. Prior to his death, the Buddha's followers were confused about his teachings and upset over not having a spiritual leader for the Saṅgha. When his favorite disciple Ānanda relayed these fears to the Buddha, he responded by saying:

> Ānanda, what does the order of the Saṅgha expect from me? I have taught the Dhamma without making any distinction as exoteric and esoteric. With regard to the truth, the Tathāgata has nothing like the closed fist of a teacher. Surely, Ānanda, if there is anyone who thinks

> that he will lead the Saṅgha, and that the Saṅgha should depend on him, let him set down his instructions. But the Tathāgata has no such idea. Why should he then leave instructions concerning the Saṅgha? Therefore, Ānanda, dwell making yourselves your island [support], making yourselves, not anyone else, your refuge. (Rahula 1974, p. 61)

The Buddha's parting advice to his disciples suggests his disappointment with them: they are still waiting for him to establish normative guidelines and say how the Saṅgha should be run. The Buddha's frustration is evident and understandable: he says he has not held anything back, that he has no absolute guidelines for his followers, and that he has no teachings about how everyone should practice. It seems as if his disciples have not listened to him at all, and he expresses his disappointment by saying, "What do they expect from me?"

Nevertheless, the disciples organized themselves into a community and quickly assembled the "First Council" to recite and organize the Buddha's teachings. To help memorize the teachings, the monks separated those dealing with important doctrines and expressed in story or discourse form, called *sūtras*, from those dealing with precepts and rules of the monastic life, called *vinaya*. Given the stress on living within the monastic community during this time, it is not surprising that the *Vinaya-pitaka*, or "Basket of Rules," was examined with precise care. Living according to the precepts of the *vinaya* distinguished a monk from a layperson, and helped the monks live a pure Buddhist life. It was thus necessary to understand the *vinaya* and act according to its principles.

A hundred years after the Buddha's death, however, a

schism arose over the *vinaya*. Some monks were found violating certain rules, such as drinking intoxicating beverages, accepting gold and silver, taking food at the wrong time of day, and saying that an *arhat* may have sexual temptations. The "Second Council" was organized to debate these matters, but instead of resolving it the schism deepened, leading to two distinct orders or sects: the Mahāsāṃghika (or "Great Assembly") who argued for the liberalization of the Buddhist precepts, and the Sthaviravāda (or "the monks of the Great Council") who advocated a strict adherence to the rules and precepts of the *vinaya*. The liberal Mahāsāṃghika school later underwent nine more schisms, and eventually led to the development of the Mahāyāna tradition, while the conservative Sthaviravāda lineage divided into eleven different schools, collectively referred to as Nikāya, or "monastic" Buddhism (Hirakawa 1990).

Nikāya Buddhism and the Development of the Abhidharma

Nikāya Buddhism refers to the scholarly and monastic form of Buddhism that developed after the initial schism of the Second Council. Nikāya Buddhism was generally secluded within monasteries, and taught that one needed to live a monastic life in order to fully observe the precepts of the *vinaya*. Because there was a sharp division between monastic and lay life during this period, liberation was often defined in exclusive terms: an arhat's job was not to help others but to strive for individual perfection and to eliminate his own defilements. This lack of social concern led the

Mahāyāna Buddhists to degrade large segments of Nikāya Buddhism as an inferior, or "Hīnayāna" teaching.

Nevertheless, an isolated and cloistered life has its benefits, as it gave the Nikāya Buddhists the freedom to engage in an intensive philosophical analysis of Buddhist philosophy. As the Mādhyamika scholar Kenneth Inada says, this period represents one of the most important moments in Buddhist history. It was, he says:

> the most active, highly vibrant and competitive age in Buddhist history . . . . If there are high watermarks to be considered in Buddhist history, this period certainly rates a very high level, a level of great fermentation and flourishing of Buddhist thought. Ideologically speaking, no other period in Buddhist history . . . could ever match, or come up to the level of activity as recorded during this period. (Inada 1970, p. 6)

The literature that developed from this period of Buddhism is called the *abhidharma*. While organizing the Buddha's discourses into the *Sūtra-pitaka*, and the monastic rules into the *Vinaya-pitaka*, the Nikāya scholars also developed a detailed classification of all the basic doctrines scattered throughout the discourses. This process of classifying and listing the main "topics" (*mātṛkā*) of the Buddha's discourses soon became an object of commentarial and scholastic study itself, and was eventually compiled into a collection called the *abhidharma-pitaka*, making up the "Three Baskets" (*Tripiṭaka*) of the early Buddhist canon.

Even though the *abhidharma* texts are conceptually dense and difficult to follow, it is clear that, like every major Buddhist tradition, the central issue is meditation and religious praxis. The detailed lists or "matrixes," the analysis of experience into *dharmas*, the examination of causal conditioning, and the emphasis on "discerning" and "watching" the flow of impermanent phenomena is a reflection on the nature of meditative practice and how it relates to liberation. The body of literature called *abhidharma* was developed for meditative praxis, and the different "sects" or schools that arose from this literature are different reflections on the proper ways to achieve *nirvāṇa*. The debates between the different schools are therefore less about doctrinal issues than about religious methodology and discipline. How many *dharmas* does one need to "discern" in meditative practice? How should one view the flow of phenomena within the stream of consciousness? The issue in these questions is soteriological and metapractical, and arises out of concern about the efficacy of the practices presented in the *abhidharma* literature.

Central to all the major Abhidharma traditions is a classification of *dharmas* into "lists" or "matrixes" (*mātṛkā*) for the purpose of meditation. While the traditions differed over the number of *mātṛkā* and number of *dharmas*, a common system was to divide the *dharmas* into three major categories: the five aggregates (*skandhas*), the twelve bases of cognition (*āyatana*), and the eighteen elements (*dhātu*). This system allowed for quick recognition of the major categories of experience that could then be sub-divided for closer analysis. The aggregate form (*rūpa*), for instance—which includes the five sense organs and five sense objects—is divided into different types of sensual experience, such as colors, sounds, tastes, smells and so on, each of which is further subdivided into the types of colors, sounds, tastes, smells, that one experiences. In this way, the Abhidharma schools hoped to classify all experience into its elemental parts, allowing for a precise analytic meditation.

While the Abhidharma traditions differed over the exact stages one had to follow to eliminate the "defilements" (*kleśa*), they generally accepted a series of stages in which one ascends from the meditative analysis of *dharmas* to a higher wisdom (*prajñā*) based on the "cessation" of *dharmas*.

In the Sarvāstivādin tradition, the stages of the "path" are divided into three levels. First, there are the "preliminary practices" that deal with physical and mental purification; second, the "seven stages of the wise" that consist primarily of meditations on the Four Noble Truths; and third, the "seven degrees of the sage" in which a practitioner "cuts off the defilements" and realizes their "cessation." In the Theravāda tradition, the levels of practice are divided into seven stages of "purification." One moves progressively from the purification of morals, mind, views, doubts, knowledge of the correct path, knowledge of the correct method, and, finally, to the "three gates" of liberation (Hirakawa 1990).

As with most Abhidharma traditions, the basis of this "correct path" is the *dharmic* analysis of experience which, as Vasubandhu said, must be "investigated" in order to "pacify the passions." Because the *dharmas* are "defiled" by desire, lust, anger, greed, ignorance, and so forth, they must be purified and eliminated. Thus, as practitioners progress through the different stages of meditation, they cultivate the insight (*vipaśyanā*) that eliminates the "defilements" and, once this is completed, attain complete emancipation.

The type of reflection we find in the Abhidharma tradition is what Kasulis calls "metapraxis" (Kauslis 1992). It is specifically concerned with how a meditation on the nature of *dharmas* will lead to liberation. "What happens after attaining the level of 'cessation' in which *dharmas* no longer arise?" "How is the stream of mental events brought to a halt through meditative practice?" "What is the relation between the 'pacification' of *dharmas* and liberation?" These questions are quite different from the types of metaphysical issues that we find in traditional Western philosophy, and should therefore make us skeptical about the claim put forth by many Western scholars that the Abhidharma is doing metaphysics, or that it is offering a theory of linguistic reference, logical atomism, or realism. It should make us even more skeptical (as we will see in Chapter 4) that Nāgārjuna is attacking the Abhidharma Buddhists on metaphysical grounds as well.

What does make the Abhidharma problematic, however, and is why the Mahāyāna tradition developed the doctrine of *upāya* in the first place, is its view that liberation entails following a fixed meditative routine. Without understanding how *dharmas* arise and cease, how they condition other things, and how they are related through subtle relays of causes and effects, one cannot attain liberation. Vasubandhu reflects this opinion in his *Abhidharmakośa* when he says:

> Because there is no means of pacifying the passions without close investigation of existents, and because it is the passions that cause the world to wander in this great ocean of transmigration, therefore they say that the teacher—which means the Buddha—spoke this system aimed at the close examination of existents. For a student is not able to closely investigate existents without teaching in true doctrine. (Pruden 1988, p. 57)

The "close investigation" that Vasubandhu mentions refers to a particular meditation on the nature of *dharmas*, a reflection that is aware of their impermanent, causal, and selfless status. He is also saying that without meditating in a particular way—i.e., without "reviewing" the Sarvāstivādin analysis of *dharmas*—it is impossible to attain liberation. In this sense, Vasubandhu is establishing the necessary conditions for practice, and, in line with many of the Abhidharma thinkers, creating an orthopraxis for all Buddhists to follow.

The Abhidharma Analysis of *Dharmas*

Although the Abhidharma schools say the Buddha taught the Abhidharma analysis of experience, it is more likely a continuation and development of important teachings from the early discourses. In reaction to the Hindu notion of an indestructible and eternal soul (*ātman*), for example, the Buddha taught his doctrine of *anātman*, or non-self, which was meant to counteract the incessant quest for a mysteriously hidden "self." According to the doctrine of *anātman*, there is no hidden or unchanging "self" that lies behind our experience. Rather, our experiences are composed of ever-changing and interdependent psychophysical forces, or aggregates (*skandhas*), with no underlying substance (*ātman*) or unifying essence. The reason for limiting the *skandhas* to five is explained by the *Visuddhi-Magga* in the following way:

> Why did The Blessed One say there were five groups, no less and no more?
>
> Because these sum up and classify, according to their

> affinities, all the constituents of being; because it is only these that can afford a basis for the figment of a Self or of anything related to a Self; and because these include all other classifications.
>
> For in classifying, according to their affinities, the many different constituents of being, form constitutes one group, and comprises everything that has any affinity to form; sensation constitutes another group, and comprises everything that has any affinity to sensation. Similarly with respect to perception and the rest. Accordingly he laid down only five groups, because these sum up and classify, according to their affinities, all the constituents of being. (*Visuddhi-Magga*, trans. by Warren 1974, p. 156–157)

According to the Abhidharma view of *anātman*, the idea of an unchanging substance or "self" is nothing but a projection onto an interdependent flux of experience. The *skandhas*, on the other hand, are impermanent features of experience, and any attempt to grasp some part of it, such as consciousness, or search for something independent of it, such as a soul, was said to be the main cause of suffering in life (*duḥkha*). It was thus vital in early Buddhism to uproot a fictitious sense of self, and is why early Buddhist texts are full of statements such as: "A particular thing is not one's Self (when it can be said that) this thing is not mine (*mama*), I am not this thing, or this thing is not my self" (Conze 1967, p. 43). A Buddhist practitioner is thus asked to be forever vigilant against attributing a "self" to any aspect of experience, always mindful of the simple flow of phenomena that rise and fall like an "empty" stream.

The *abhidharma* literature was created to aid this

meditative process. It analyzed the *skandhas* into finer elements, creating ever more subtle distinctions for the purpose of sorting out, and being able to quickly recognize, the complex phenomenal threads involved in any experience. For example, the five *skandhas* can easily be broken down and divided into a more accurate account of the different types of feelings that accompany a sensation, or the different types of colors or sounds involved in a particular perceptual event, or the different kinds of ideas that take place in an act of conscious awareness. These different types of experience were labeled *dharmas*, or elements of experience, and constitute the phenomenal world. As Hirakawa explains it:

> The five aggregates of which a person is composed (form, sensation, perception, mental formations, and consciousness) are considered to be *dharmas*. However, the aggregates of form (*rūpa*) and mental phenomena (*saṃskāra*) can be further classified and subdivided into additional *dharmas*. *Rūpa* refers to both the body and material objects. For the body, five *dharmas* referring to the five senses are listed: eye, ear, nose, tongue, and body.... The material of the external world is also divided into five categories that are the objects of sense perception: forms, sounds, smells, tastes, and tangible objects. Here, *rūpa* refers to visual objects, things with form and color. Such objects of vision are further divided into categories of color such as blue, yellow, red, and white. Each of these elements exists as a *dharma*. Sounds, smells, tastes, and tangible objects are also analyzed further into basic units. (Hirakawa 1990, p. 47)

The *dharmas*, however, are not unchanging or eternal: they are impermanent, and rise and fall through the process of "dependent origination." This practice of dividing and analyzing experience into a finely knit grid of *dharmas* is supposed to help a practitioner reflect on the causal flow of experience. For someone struck by emotional pain, for example, the *dharma* theory can act as a medicinal aid. By labeling that emotion as a *dharma* of "pain" one can realize that, like all *dharmas* of this type, it is conditioned by other *dharmas*, such as those dealing with memories, mental formations, physiological sensations, and so forth, and that because it is impermanent there is no need to fixate on it. Seeing it as "conditioned" and "impermanent" results from labeling it a *dharma*, and is supposed to act as a barrier against positing it in a fixed or substantial way. One can simply "watch" it rise and fall without being attached to it in a consuming manner. All mental and physical experiences are to be viewed in this manner, and any reification of a false sense of "self" dissolves away into currents of sensations, impressions, feelings, and ideas—with no underlying substrate and, hence, no "thing" to become attached to.

As a meditation device, it is clear how much the *abhidharma* literature resembles the Buddha's counsel to think of his teachings as "rafts." The analytical technique of this tradition can help one experience life as deeply inter-connected, fully conditioned, and impermanent. As Herbert Guenther says:

> The *abhidharma*, however dry its presentation in a highly technical language may appear to us at first sight, aims at nothing less than to open man's eyes to

> that which is not speculatively arrived at by the logical method of hypothesis and deductive verification, but which can be immediately apprehended and is applicable to ourselves. (Guenther 1976, p. 3)

The Tibetan Buddhist Chogyam Trungpa makes a similar observation in his *Glimpses of the Abhidharma*:

> It is helpful not only for pure meditation but also meditation in action. The whole approach of Buddhism is oriented towards dealing with everyday life situations . . . [it is] concerned with how to step out of our usual sleepwalking and deal really with actual situations. The abhidharma is a very important part of that general instruction. (Trungpa 1978, p. 3)

The dominant trend in Abhidharma Buddhism saw it differently, however. Even though the *abhidharma* literature was first construed as another skillful means to aid meditative practice, it soon overcame this "lower" status and was transformed into the Buddha's "ultimate" or "literal" discourses. As Paul Griffiths puts it:

> The result of a consistent and determined effort to internalize the categories of Buddhist thought by way of the practice of analytic meditation is, it is said, identical with the removal of ignorance, the attainment of knowledge, and the development of the ability to perceive things as they really are. When this accurate knowledge and clear perception is continuously pos-

> sessed by the practitioner, the root cause of bondage is removed and salvation attained. (Griffiths 1986, p. 14)

Mindfulness, or *smṛti*, consists in "getting *dharmas* into view" for the Abhidharma Buddhists, in isolating them, reflecting on them, and "burning" them up. While this process requires great meditative skill, the Abhidharma philosophers struggled to articulate what actually happens during the higher forms of meditation. Given their claim that everyone needs to meditate on impermanence, for instance, it became difficult for them to map out the precise manner in which *dharmas* actually change. Stcherbatsky hints at the problem in his description of *dharmas*:

> The elements of existence are momentary appearances, momentary flashings into the phenomenal world out of an unknown source .... They disappear as soon as they appear, in order to be followed in the next moment by another momentary existence. Thus a moment becomes a synonym of an element (*dharma*), two moments are two different elements. An element becomes something like a point in time-space .... Consequently, the elements do not change, but disappear, the world becomes a cinema. Disappearance is the essence of existence; what does not disappear does not exist. (Stcherbatsky 1961, p. 32)

While Stcherbatsky sees the problem of *dharmas* as a metaphysical problem, his comments highlight a central issue in the Abhidharma tradition. If all *dharmas* are "momentary" units of experience, as everyone in this tradition holds, then how are we supposed to explain the relationship between one *dharmic* moment and the next? Even the Vedānta philosopher Śaṅkara saw this problem when he examined the issue of causality in relation to "momentary" existence:

> Those who maintain that everything has a momentary existence only admit that when the thing existing in the second moment enters into being, the thing existing in the first moment ceases to be. On this admission, it is impossible to establish between the two things the relation of cause and effect, since the former momentary existence ceases or has ceased to be, and so has entered into the state of non-existence, and cannot be the cause of the later momentary existence. (Radhakrishnan 1973, p. 235)

The Abhidharma Buddhists were also aware of this problem, and tried to fix it by coming up with different theories to explain how *dharmas* interact causally. The Sarvāstivādins tried to distinguish between the substance of a *dharma* (*svabhāva*) and its causal properties, saying that even though a *dharma's* properties change, its substance remains the same, while the Sautrāntika and Theravāda traditions developed theories that Kalupahana calls "immediate contiguity," in other words, theories that locate causality in some form of immediate connection.

While this problem of causality may seem excessively abstract and obscure, it has serious soteriological implications for the Abhidharma thinkers. They are not simply quenching their metaphysical thirst or speculating on the causal structure of the universe. Rather, they are seeking liberation from a *dharmic* world. Given their view that conditioned *dharmas* are "defiled" by lust, anger, and ignorance, the problem is how to escape this world and enter into something unconditioned and undefiled: in other words, *nirvāṇa*. The following two sections will explore this problem in more detail, focusing on the issue of causality in two of the most important Abhidharma schools, the Sarvāstivādin and Sautrāntika.

Causality in the Sarvāstivādin Tradition

In attempting to reconcile the theory of *dharmas* with the doctrines of impermanence, the Sarvāstivādin philosophers borrowed the idea of causal identity from the Hindu Sāṅkhya tradition. According to the Sāṅkhya philosopher Īśhvarakṛṣṇa, causes and effects are identical because both are united by the same primordial "stuff" or substance, *prakṛti*. The changes we see in the world are nothing but the unfolding of this self-same substance, and even though the characteristics of *prakṛti* undergo change, *prakṛti* in itself remains the same. As Īśhvarakṛṣṇa says,

> The qualities of Nature have an unmanifested entity for their cause [i.e., they have a cause in which they exist in their unmanifested state]—because they are finite—like the jar and other things—the jar and other things are found to have, for their cause, clay and other things, in which inhere the unmanifested state of the effects. (*Sāṅkhya-kārikā*, quoted in Radhakrishnan 1973, p. 426)

The Sarvāstivādin philosophers made a similar distinction between the substance of a thing and its characteristics, and said that even though a *dharma's* characteristics change, its intrinsic nature (*svabhāva*) remains unaltered. Similar to Īśhvarakṛṣṇa, they proposed a view of causal identity, and said that a *dharma's* "own nature" (*svabhāva*) remains through the three time periods. Stcherbatsky tries to explain this in the following way:

> All elements exist on two different planes, the real essence of the element (*svabhāva-dharma*) and its momentary manifestation. The first exists always, in past, present, and future; . . . it represents the potential appearances of the element into phenomenal existence, and its past appearances as well. (Stcherbatsky 1961, p. 35)

According to the Sarvāstivādins, one only recognizes a *dharma* in its present manifest form by its "mark" or *lakṣaṇa*. Its real existence, however, is something that lasts through time, and even though its manifest "mark" changes according to the law's impermanence, its essence endures throughout a particular moment in which a *dharma* arises, abides, and then decays.

The *Abhidharmakośa* refers to four causal theories of the Sarvāstivādin tradition. The philosopher Dharmatrāta argued that a *dharma*, while existing throughout the three time periods of past, present, and future, changes its state (*bhāva*) but not its underlying substance; Ghoṣaka argued that only the characteristics of a thing are subject to change, and that it "retains" its aspects from every time period;

Vasumitra said that as an element passes through the three time periods it changes its conditions; and Buddhadeva said that a thing changes only in relation to things past, present, and future.

Vasubandhu notes that only the third view—arguing for a change in condition but not in substance—was widely accepted in Sarvāstivādin circles. Nevertheless, all four theories share the same basic assumption that a *dharma* can be divided into "two spheres," one part exists in time and connects with other manifested *dharmas*, and the other part is substantially distinct. Underlying the causal process, which is but a "conventional" designation for fleeting appearances, is the self-same substance that resides "over" time.

While it may appear that the Sarvāstivādins are engaged in metaphysics, they are actually struggling with a metapractical problem. Their "substantialistic" account of *dharmas* is an attempt to account for the continuity of "defiled" *dharmas*. Even though *dharmas* are supposedly impermanent, it was obvious to the Sarvāstivādin philosophers that "past" *dharmas* influence or "contaminate" present experience, such that past anger, lust, and ignorance condition what happens now as well as in the future. In other words, "defiled" *dharmas* set the stage for action (*karma*), and these actions are then repeated—or "reborn"—throughout the three time periods.

Dharmas are therefore a highly complicated and dangerous affair for the Sarvāstivādin thinkers: complicated because they go through change and yet endure, and dangerous because their substantive element—their "self-nature"—continues through experience, making them extremely difficult to "burn up" and destroy. In fact, "defiled" *dharmas* are so substantial for the Sarvāstivādins that liberation is almost impossible to attain, for once the stream of experience is "defiled" it continues without stopping.

Because of the precarious nature of "defiled" *dharmas*, the Sarvāstivādins said that one had to meditate on the unconditioned (*nirvāṇa*) in order to attain release. Since the "defiled" *dharmas* are so "substantial" there is no way to halt their activity except by submitting oneself to a "correct" form of meditation that will "interrupt" the causal process, allowing for the possibility of an unconditioned experience. A "pure" *dharma* such as *nirvāṇa*, for example, is unconditioned, it is not caused or produced, and it exists independently from the causal activity of our "everyday" world. But in order to experience this one must disrupt the causal process so that "defiled" *dharmas* are destroyed. Personal identity is then completely "interrupted," and one would be released from a conditioned world in which "defiled" *dharmas* repeat themselves indefinitely. As we will see in Chapter 3, this metapractical justification for a particular form of meditation found in the *abhidharma* literature pitted the Sarvāstivādins against a newly emerging Mahāyāna tradition.

Causality in the Sautrāntika Tradition

The Sautrāntika philosophers rejected the Sarvāstivādin conception of *svabhāva* because it contradicts the doctrine of *anātman* by positing abiding substances. They also found the division of *dharmas* into substance and properties an absurd distinction that only confuses our ability to explain impermanence:

> They cannot explain the origination and decay [which are going on in the process of life]. An element, according to this view, is permanent and impermanent at the same time. This indeed, is something quite new! (Stcherbatsky 1973, p. 72)

The Sautrāntika criticism of the Sarvāstivādin was relatively straightforward. To say that the past, present, and future endure over time or exist in some substantial manner not only confuses the relationship between these three periods, but makes our everyday understanding of these terms impossible:

> If they are always existent, how is the [remarkable result] brought about that they are called past or future? Therefore, the words of our Sublime Lord, "there *is* a past, there *is* a future," must be understood in another sense. He proffered them when discussing with the Ajivikas [who denied moral responsibility for past deeds]. He strongly opposed their doctrine, which denied the connexion between a past cause and a future result. In order to make it known that a former cause and a future are something which happened formerly and will happen in the future, he categorically declared: "there *is* a past, there *is* a future." For the word "is" acts as a particle [which may refer to something existent and to non-existent as well]. As, for example, people will say: "there *is* absence of light [before it has been kindled], "there *is* absence of light [it has been put out]," or the "light *is* put out, but I did not put it out." When Buddha declared that there "is" a past and there "is" a future, he

> used the word "is" in that sense. Had it been otherwise, it would be absolutely impossible to account for [the notions of] a past and a future. (Stcherbatsky 1973, p. 73)

Even though the Sautrāntika denied the idea of *svabhāva* as simply another form of *ātman*, they nevertheless accepted the theory of "moments" common to all the Abhidharma traditions, and were thus faced with the same dilemma of explaining the continuity between two *dharmic* moments. They confronted this dilemma in two ways: first, by saying that only the present moment exists, thus denying any substantial reality to the past and future; and second, by saying that the present "moment" is nothing else but the "coming into" and "going out of" existence. In other words, all things are characterized by birth and death such that what is born comes out of nothing and what dies goes into nothing. Rather than seeing *dharmas* develop from their "own nature," as in the Sarvastivadin tradition, the Sautrāntikas argue that a *dharma* is simply a "continuous flow" in a whole series of successive moments. Thus, what appears static, or what seems like a change of a single substance, is just the continual creation—and immediate destruction—of new *dharmas*. As Vasubandhu explains it:

> When the organ of vision [eye] is produced, it does not come from some other place; when it disappears it is not going to be stored up in another place. [Consequently] a thing becomes, having not been before; having become, it ceases to be. (Pruden p. 219)

Kalupahana explains this by saying that birth is the beginning of a *dharmic* series, decay the transition into a new *dharma* within the series, and destruction the final end of the series altogether. The causation of each individual moment, he says, is therefore reduced to "invariable antecedence" (Kalupahana 1975, p. 151). It is not clear exactly what this means, and Mookerjee is probably right when he says, "From the elaborate exposition of the theory of causation with its confused tangle of criticism and counter criticism . . . one cannot resist the impression that the Sautrāntika has failed, in spite of his logical acumen and wealth of dialectic, to carry any conviction" (quoted in Kalupahana 1975, p. 152).

Summary

It is important to pause and reflect on why the Abhidharma traditions are debating over causality. To say they are concerned with the metaphysics of causality—as if they simply want a clearer picture of the universe—would distort their project by framing the issue in terms of what we can and cannot know about the world. But the issue for the Abhidharma is not an issue of knowledge, and is not about objectively describing what happens "out there" in the world. Rather, like most Buddhist traditions, the fundamental issue is liberation and the proper ways to meditate. By developing systematic accounts of *dharmas* and dividing them into "martixes" of experiences, the Abhidharma is engaged in a metapractical reflection on the nature of Buddhist practice, and is trying to philosophically justify how one *should* meditate in order to attain liberation. The issue is not only what constitutes orthopraxis in the Buddhist tradition, but which practice works and why. Given that causality is a central mediation practice in each of these traditions, it should be obvious why the philosophers of this tradition devote so much intellectual energy to how *dharmas* rise and cease, and it should be obvious that what distinguishes these traditions has little to do with theories of causation apart from Buddhist meditation.

However, even though the Abhidharma traditions offer different metapractical theories on how to meditate on the *Abhidharma* texts, they come together by insisting that one *must* meditate in a particular way to attain liberation. Such orthopraxic measures spurred the creation of the Mahāyāna tradition in Buddhism, which responded with a massive array of philosophical texts and scriptures directly challenging Abhidharma Buddhism. As we will see in the following chapter, Mahāyāna texts such as the *Lotus Sūtra*, *Prajñāpāramitā*, and *Vimalakīrtinirdeśa* criticize the Abhidharma for restricting Buddhism to a fixed path, and argue that all of the Buddha's teachings—including *nirvāṇa*, "dependent arising," and "emptiness"—are nothing more than "skill-in-means."

Chapter 3

Mahāyāna Buddhism: The *Vimalakīrtinirdeśa*

Introduction

The term Mahāyāna or "Great Vehicle" was coined in reaction to the Scholastic Buddhist tradition, which was labeled a Hīnayāna or "Lesser Vehicle." Although we are not exactly sure when the Mahāyāna first developed, a new style of writing emerged sometime during the first century B.C.E. that differed dramatically from the *abhidharma* literature. Whereas the *abhidharma* is famous for its prosaic style, logical precision, and detailed analysis, the new Mahāyāna tradition developed a literary style that is rich in the use of metaphor, religious symbolism, and magical events. Even a cursory glance at any of the early Mahāyāna texts shows that a major literary shift has taken place.

The *Lotus Sūtra*, for example, begins with a mythological story of the Buddha sitting in meditation surrounded by monks, bodhisattvas, Nāgas, animals, and thousands of divine and semidivine beings, all participating in a miraculous event:

> And as the Lord had entered upon his meditation, there fell a great rain of divine flowers covering the Lord and the four classes of hearers, while the whole Buddha field shook in six ways; it moved, removed, trembled, trembled from one end to the other, tossed along.

> Then did those who were assembled and sitting together in that congregation, monks, nuns, male and female lay devotees, gods, Nāgas, goblins, demons, great serpents, men, and beings not human, as well as rulers of armies and rulers of four continents, all of them with their followers, gaze on the Lord in astonishment, in amazement, in ecstasy.
> And at that moment there issued a ray from within the circle of hair between the eyebrows of the Lord. It extended over eighteen hundred thousand Buddha fields in the eastern quarter, so that all those Buddha fields appeared wholly illuminated by its radiance, down to the great hell and up to the limit of existence. And the beings in any of the six states of existence became visible, all without exception. (Kern 1989, p. 4-6)

This mythological vision of the Buddha is prevalent in most Mahāyāna sūtras from this time on, and is a clear break from the analytic prose of the *abhidharma* texts. This shift in emphasis is more than a mere literary transition, however, and points to a critical debate between the Mahāyāna and Abhidharma traditions. As discussed in the previous chapter, the Abhidharma schools elevated the *abhidharma* texts to the "highest" teachings of Buddhism and reduced the notion of "skillful means" to a single meditation praxis. The Mahāyāna tradition reversed this trend by labeling the Abhidharma philosophy a Hīnayāna or "inferior" teaching, and placed "skillful means" on the forefront by making it the highest spiritual practice of a bodhisattva's life. The *Perfection of Wisdom* (*Prajñāpāramitā*) sūtras place it alongside *prajñā*, or "wisdom," and the famous Mādhyamika philosopher Nāgārjuna sees it as the "father" of bodhisattvic activity: "Prajñāpāramitā is the mother of Bodhisattvas, skill-in-means is their father, and compassion is their daughter" (Lindtner 1986, p. 128). Likewise, in place of the *arhat* who supposedly strives for his own liberation, the Mahāyāna promotes the bodhisattva, the "enlightened being" who rejects the "selfish" individualism of the *arhats* and devotes himself to helping others. What distinguishes the bodhisattvas perhaps more than anything is their ability to use an endless number of skillful means to help human beings cross the turbulent waters of *saṁsāra*.

Moreover, the *Lotus Sūtra* tells us that everything contained in its pages is nothing more than an *upāya*:

> I have attained the Buddha-way, and making use of skillful means I proclaim this sūtra so that they [sentient beings] may abide in it. (Kern 1989, p. 285)

The doctrine of *upāya* thus signifies much more than a literary transition for the Mahāyāna tradition, and refers to a reinterpretation of all the major philosophical and religious terms used by the early Buddhists. Even the most cherished idea of *nirvāṇa*—which the Abhidharma Buddhists spent so much time "reviewing"—is now just one of the many pedagogical "devices" used in Buddhism. As it says in the *Lotus Sūtra*:

> To those [who are suffering] I show a device [*upāya*] and say: put an end to your trouble. When I perceive creatures vexed with mishap I make them see Nirvāṇa. (Kern 1989, p. 46)

To explain the importance of skillful means in the Mahāyāna tradition, this chapter will focus primarily on one text, the *Vimalakīrtinirdeśa*. This important text covers all the major philosophical concepts used in Buddhist philosophy, such as "emptiness," the doctrine of "two-truths," the "three marks" of existence, and the doctrine of *upāya*. However, what separates it from other Mahāyāna texts is the way it attacks the Abhidharma tradition. Already familiar with the early Buddhist metaphor of the "raft," the *Vimalakīrtinirdeśa* refers to the Dharma as a great narrative the Buddha recounts to people. According to the *Vimalakīrtinirdeśa*, the Buddha is a great storyteller, and he weaves his medicinal rafts through fictional devices that captivate his audience. In fact, everything the Buddha teaches is a story, according to this sūtra, and we are advised to pay attention to both the storyteller and the audience to fully appreciate what is being said.

The *Vimalakīrtinirdeśa* Sūtra

As with most early sūtras, nothing definite is known about who wrote the *Vimalakīrtinirdeśa* or when it was composed, although it claims to record events surrounding the life of the historical Buddha. Most scholars place it after the *Perfection of Wisdom* (*Prajñāpāramitā*) sūtras, sometime around 100 C.E.

The main character in the text is a man named Vimalakīrti, described as a person who embodies the highest virtues of Buddhist life. Vimalakīrti is neither a monk living a life of piety nor a bodhisattva, however, but a layman who enjoys the pleasures of daily life. He has a wife and son, engages in business, and spends his time with ordinary people such as gamblers, warriors, government officials, businesspeople, prostitutes, and so forth. Nevertheless, he excels in all the Buddhist virtues:

> Having served the ancient Buddhas, he had generated the roots of virtue by honoring them and making offerings to them. He had attained tolerance as well as eloquence. He played with the great superknowledges. He had attained the power of incantations and the fearlessnesses. He had conquered all demons and opponents. He had penetrated the profound way of the Dharma. He was liberated through the transcendence of wisdom. Having integrated his realization with skill in liberative technique, he was expert in knowing the thoughts and actions of living beings. Knowing the strength or weakness of their faculties, and being gifted with unrivaled eloquence, he taught the Dharma appropriately to each . . . . He lived with the deportment of a Buddha, and his superior intelligence was as wide as the ocean. (*Vimalakīrtinirdeśa* trans. by Thurman 1986, p. 20)

Vimalakīrti's ability to experience the depths of Buddhist wisdom without retreating into otherworldly contemplation expresses the engaged, "worldly" ethics of Mahāyāna Buddhism, and is an example of how to integrate wisdom (*prajñā*) with "skill-in-means." In fact, as Vimalakīrti says, wisdom without "skill-in-means" is bondage:

> Wisdom not integrated with liberative technique is bondage, but wisdom integrated with liberative technique is liberation. (Thurman 1986, p. 46)

What does Vimalakīrti mean by saying that wisdom without "skillful means" is bondage? It means that even though a practitioner has mastered the techniques that lead to wisdom, he nevertheless remains attached to those very practices, and is therefore stuck in *saṁsāra*. As Vimalakīrti says:

> It means that a bodhisattva disciplines himself in the teachings of emptiness . . . . and brings on the development of living beings, but all the time has a mind full of clinging views. This is called the bondage of insight without skillful means. (Thurman 1986, p. 47)

As Michael Pye notes, the "clinging views" Vimalakīrti mentions here are not as deplorable as they might seem, since they are, after all, those very meditative disciplines that lead to love and compassion (Pye 1978, p. 98). However, despite the bodhisattva's noble intention to liberate human beings, he is nevertheless attached to those very practices that are supposed to help him. Even though he is disciplined in the "teachings of emptiness," for example, he is unable to help others due to his clinging, and his wisdom is therefore limited. As Vimalakīrti notes, without integrating "skill-in-means" the bodhisattva will never experience the type of "emptiness" that leads to compassion.

Vimalakīrti's demand to integrate "skill-in-means" with wisdom is a direct criticism of the Abhidharma Buddhists. Even though they have "mastered" all the religious disciplines and meditation practices, and even though they are "experts" in Buddhist logic and analysis, they mistake meditation for ritualized behavior, and wisdom for rote doctrine. Vimalakīrti singles out Śāriputra as a representative of this "Hīnayāna" problem when he tells him:

> Reverend Śāriputra, he who is interested in the Dharma has no interest in matter, sensation, intellect, motivation, or consciousness. He has no interest in these aggregates, or in the elements, or in the sense-media. Interested in the Dharma, he has no interest in the realm of desire, the realm of matter, or the immaterial realm. Interested in the Dharma, he is not interested in attachment to the Buddha, attachment to the Dharma, or attachment to the Saṇgha. (Thurman 1986, p. 50)

The aggregates, elements and sense-media Vimalakīrti mentions refer to the Abhidharma analysis of experience and the specific "path" one needs to follow for liberation. While these ideas were originally devised to help Buddhists attain wisdom and compassion, they have nevertheless become a source of bondage because they lack the assistance of *upāya*.

In Chapters 3 and 4, Vimalakīrti chastises the Buddha's immediate disciples and bodhisattvas for becoming attached to Buddhist doctrine. They preach Buddhism indiscriminately, and speak to others without taking into account their spiritual, emotional, and intellectual levels. But the Dharma "is not a secure refuge," says Vimalakīrti, and "without examining the spiritual faculties of living beings one can wound those who are without wounds" (Thurman 1986, p. 28). In these and later chapters, Vimalakīrti interrupts the speeches of the disciples and scolds them for being disconnected from their audience. When the Buddha asks his disciple Pūrṇa to go visit Vimalakīrti and inquire about his illness, for example, Pūrṇa responds with the following story:

> Lord, I am indeed reluctant to go to this good man to inquire about his illness. Why? Lord, I remember one day, when I was teaching the Dharma to some young monks in the great forest, the Licchaavi Vimalakīrti came there and said to me, "Reverend Pūrṇa, first concentrate yourself, regard the minds of these young bhikṣus, and then teach them the Dharma! Do not put rotten food into a jeweled bowl! First understand the inclinations of these monks, and do not confuse priceless sapphires with glass beads!" (Thurman 1986, p. 28)

Vimalakīrti repeats these harsh words to all the other disciples and bodhisattvas, condemning them for their attachments to Buddhism, their arrogance, and their dispassionate relationship with others. Understandably, the disciples and bodhisattvas are reluctant to see Vimalakīrti ever again on account of his harsh tone with those who preach without integrating "skillful means." As Pūrṇa says, "It occurred to me then, 'The disciples, who do not know the thoughts or the inclinations of others, are not able to teach the Dharma to anyone.' " (Thurman 1986, p. 29)

Vimalakīrti's criticism of this type of attachment has a long history in Buddhism, and is continued in China by the Ch'an master Lin-chi:

> Followers of the Way, here and there you hear it is said that there is a Way to be practiced, a Dharma to

> become enlightened to. Will you tell me then just what Dharma there is to become enlightened to, what Way there is to practice? . . . There are a bunch of bald-headed monks who tell students of the Way that the Way represents the ultimate goal, and that one must spend three *asamkhya kalpas* carrying out and fulfilling all the religious practices before one can gain complete understanding of the Way . . . [but] don't take the Buddha to be some sort of ultimate goal. In my view he's more like the hole in a privy. Bodhisattvas and arhats are all so many cangues and chains, things for fettering people . . . . Followers of the Way, there is no Buddha to be gained, and the Three Vehicles, the five natures, the teachings of perfect and immediate enlightenment are all simply medicines to cure diseases of the moment. (Watson 1993, p. 48-76)

Similar to Lin-chi's attack on those who cling to Buddhism, Vimalakīrti warns the disciples and bodhisattvas that attachment to Buddhism stands in the way of compassion. When Pūrṇa says that those "who do not know the thoughts or the inclinations of others are not able to teach the Dharma to anyone," he learns that Buddhist wisdom involves a deep intimacy with others, and that there is more to being a bodhisattva than simply knowing the bare "truths" of suffering, "non-self," and impermanence. In short, he learns that one must know others before engaging in any Dharma discourse.

The "Three Marks" of Existence

When we first meet Vimalakīrti, he is giving a speech about suffering to a group of villagers who live in his area:

> Friends, this body is so impermanent, fragile, unworthy of confidence, and feeble. It is so insubstantial, perishable, short-lived, painful, filled with diseases, and subject to changes . . . . It is like a magical illusion, consisting of falsifications. It is like a dream, being an unreal vision. It is like a reflection, being the image of former actions. It is like an echo, being dependent on conditions . . . . Therefore, you should be repulsed by such a body. (Thurman 1986, p. 8)

Vimalakīrti's discourse mirrors the Buddha's doctrine of *duḥkha*, and seems to be spoken in a very literal sense. The body, which includes almost every aspect of experiential life, is inherently contaminated and should be seen as repulsive. It is *duḥkha*. "What terrors are we not exposed to by the mere fact of having a body!" says Conze, commenting on the doctrine of *duḥkha*. "Much pleasure is followed by bad karmic consequences (punishment), and by fresh craving which ties us to this world" (Conze 1967, p. 74). The body is "short lived" and impermanent, it is an "echo" without substance, and an "image" that bears the fruit of all past conditioning. Therefore, says Vimalakīrti, we should be repulsed by it.

This is the Buddha's First Noble Truth, that says all conditioned phenomena share three "marks" or characteristics (*lakṣaṇa*). All experience, said the Buddha, is (1) impermanent (*anitya*), (2) ill (*duḥkha)*, and (3) non-substantial (*anātman*). The three *lakṣaṇa* are so basic to Buddhist thought that every introductory Buddhist text refers to them in one way or another, and Vimalakīrti's treatment of them appears, at least on a superficial level, very traditional. He simply recounts what the Buddha already said, and what every Buddhist practitioner already knows. However, there is also something distinctly "unorthodox" in Vimalakīrti's treatment of the *lakṣaṇa,* something that reveals just how non-doctrinal his position really is. Before examining what this is, however, we need a clear view of how the "three marks" are understood in Buddhism.

The first "mark" of existence is impermanence (*anitya*), and expresses the basic Buddhist world-view. When we analyze our experience we supposedly never find anything that is unaltered from one moment to the next. As the Abhidharma tradition held, all *dharmas* are born, remain for an instant, and then die almost as soon as they arise, leaving nothing but a continuous flow of experiential events that rise and cease at every instance. And yet, like Vimalakīrti, the Buddha says that whatever is impermanent should be treated as ill and therefore rejected: "What is impermanent, that is not worth delighting in, not worth being impressed by, not worth clinging to." One should not even try to cling to impermanent phenomena because they are associated with suffering, *duḥkha*, the second "mark." As the Buddha says:

> Now this, O monks, is the noble truth of *duḥkha*: birth is painful, old age is painful, sickness is painful, death is painful, sorrow, lamentation, dejection, and despair are painful. Contact with the unpleasant is painful, not getting what one wishes is painful. In short, the five *skandhas* of grasping are painful. (Warren 1986, p. 47)

Because ordinary experience is "marked" by the process of birth, decay, and death—i.e., impermanence—it is connected to pain and should be rejected. Long before Vimalakīrti, the Buddha taught that we should cultivate a sense of disgust with impermanence because it is full of pain and suffering. "In short," says the Buddha, "the five *skandhas* of grasping are painful," and he recommends that we cultivate a sense of aversion for the eye and the impressions it receives, the ear and sounds, the nose and odors, the body and tangible things, and so on. "This body," says Vimalakīrti, echoing the Buddha, "is filthy, being an agglomeration of pus and excrement. Therefore, you should be repulsed by such a body." (Thurman 1986, p. 22)

The third "mark" of existence is "non-self" or *anātman*. All of life, says Vimalakīrti, is "insubstantial . . . like a water bubble . . . selfless, like water . . . and nonsubstantial, like space" (Thurman 1986, p. 22). There is nothing fixed or permanent in our experiences, and it is impossible to discover a substantial "self" in the world. Instead, all things are dependently related through a process of conditioning, always "turbulent" and changing. Because of this, Buddhists say that life is "non-substantial" or *anātman*. As the Buddha says in the *Samyutta-Nikāya*:

> The body, monks, is selfless. If the body, monks, were the self, this body would not be subject to sickness, and it would be possible in the case of the body to say, "Let my body be thus, let my body not be thus." Now, because the body is soulless, monks, therefore the body is subject to sickness, and it is not possible in the case of the body to say "Let my body be thus, let my body be thus."
>
> Consciousness is soulless. For if consciousness were the soul, this consciousness would not be subject to sickness, and it would not be possible in the case of consciousness to say, "Let my consciousness be thus, let my consciousness not be thus."

> Therefore in truth, monks, whatever body, past, future, or present, internal or external, gross or subtle, low or eminent, near or far, is to be looked on by him who duly and rightly understands, as, "all this body is not mine, not this am I, not mine is the soul." (Warren 1986, p. 182).

The Buddha's argument for the "third mark" is voiced primarily against the Hindu notion of an unchanging *ātman*. If there is a "self," he says, it would have to be permanent, eternal, and "uncontaminated" by conditioned phenomena. However, neither the body nor consciousness (or any other aspect of experience) is immune from diseases, which means they are conditioned and, hence, "selfless."

How is Vimalakīrti's discussion of the three "marks" any different from the Abhidharma discussion? Is his approach any less dogmatic than their approach to the subject? The main difference between Vimalakīrti and the Abhidharma philosophers is that Vimalakīrti refuses to see the three *lakṣaṇa* as the absolutely true discourses of the Buddha. In his view, they are simply fictional "devices" rather than universal truths, and exemplify just one form of Buddhist communication.

We learn about this "fictional" status of the *lakṣaṇa* not only in what Vimalakīrti says about them, but in the very structure of the text itself. In the "Skillful Means" chapter, for instance, we are told that Vimalakīrti fakes an illness. He pretends to manifest himself as *duḥkha* so the villagers (and later in the text, the disciples and bodhisattvas) will visit him:

> At that time, out of this very skill in liberative technique [*upāya*], Vimalakīrti manifested himself as if sick. To inquire after his health, the king, the officials, the lords, the youths, the aristocrats, the householders, the businessmen, the townsfolk, the country folk, and thousands of other living beings came forth from the great city of Vaisali and called on the invalid. When they arrived, Vimalakīrti taught them the Dharma. (Thurman 1986, p. 21–22)

What he goes on to teach was already quoted above: the "truth" of *duḥkha*. But this teaching is confounded because Vimalakīrti is not being completely "truthful." He "lies" to the villagers about his sickness, and then teaches them about the nature of sickness (*duḥkha*). The connection here should be obvious. Vimalakīrti's own sickness is "fictitious": it is a ruse he employs to get the villagers to come see him. But the content of his teachings—that which refers to the three "marks" of existence—is no doubt "fictitious" in the same sense. His own sickness and his teaching about sickness turn out to be identical: both are "fictional" devices, and therefore neither is really "true." Vimalakīrti's discourse about the nature of suffering, impermanence, and nonsubstantiality, while appearing to be spoken in a literal or truthful sense, is really an *upāyic* story that makes sense only in the context of helping this particular audience. The sūtra makes this clear to us by connecting Vimalakīrti's feigned illness with his teaching on *duḥkha*, and by including this entire event within a chapter called "Skillful Means."

But why does Vimalakīrti do this? Why does he "fictionalize" an illness and offer "false" teachings? This exact question is raised by the Bodhisattva Mañjuśrī in Chapter 5, and Vimalakīrti responds by saying:

> You ask me, Mañjuśrī, whence comes my sickness; the sicknesses of the bodhisattvas arise from great compassion. (Thurman 1986, p. 43)

Vimalakīrti manifests himself as ill and teaches *duḥkha* out of compassion. He sees others suffering in life and, "out of this very skill in liberative technique," strives to help them. He does this in two ways: first, by "fictionalizing" his own sickness to bring the villagers (and then the disciples and bodhisattvas) to visit him, and then by telling a story about *duḥkha* because he thinks this particular story will help these particular people overcome their attachments. The point is that Vimalakīrti's compassion determines what he is going to say; it molds the style and content of his teaching, and not, as the Abhidharma Buddhists would have it, the other way around. One must "first know the thoughts and inclinations of others," says Vimalakīrti, before engaging in any Dharma discourse.

Because Vimalakīrti resists being attached to any single religious method or pedagogical practice, he is open to using any number of heuristic devices. "For this reason," says the Buddha in the *Lotus Sūtra*, "I use hundred thousands of various skillful means, such as different interpretations, indications, explanations, illustrations." Vimalakīrti also preaches the "Dharma appropriate to each," and promotes a variety of lifestyles, many of which go against "orthodox" Buddhist doctrine. In Chapter 8, he shocks the Buddha's disciples by proclaiming that even the most "evil" actions can be part of a bodhisattva's path:

> He may follow the ways of avarice, yet he gives away all internal and external things without regard even for his own life. He may follow the ways of wickedness and anger, yet he remains utterly free of malice and lives by love. He may follow the ways of laziness, yet his efforts are uninterrupted as he strives in the cultivation of roots of virtue. He may follow the ways of sensuous distraction, yet, naturally concentrated, his contemplation is not dissipated. He may follow the ways of false wisdom, yet, having reached the transcendence of wisdom, he is expert in all mundane and transcendental sciences. (Thurman 1986, p. 64)

As noted in Chapter 1, the Buddha is portrayed in the *Upāyakauśalya Sūtra* as practicing some of the activities suggested by Vimalakīrti. He broke his monastic vows to have sex with a young woman who was about to kill herself, and he killed a man to prevent him from murdering 500 other people. Such practices go against "orthodox" doctrine, yet suggest that Buddhist morality is itself an *upāya*. When guided by compassion, the Buddha and Bodhisattvas do whatever is necessary to help human beings.

In Vimalakīrti's hands, the three *lakṣaṇa* are recovered from an Abhidharma fixation on orthodoxy and transformed into soteriological tools that suit the particular levels of human beings. Rather than telling us how all things *must* be "selfless," impermanent, and non-substantial, and rather than saying that everyone must meditate on these "truths" in order to achieve liberation, Vimalakīrti uses the *lakṣaṇa* to instill a sense of detachment in his listeners. Given a different audience, however, and he may reject the *lakṣaṇa*; in fact, with a different audience Vimalakīirti may even teach views that "contradict" the orthodox Buddhist position regarding the "selfless" and impermanent nature of experience. Nāgārjuna makes a similar point in his *Mādhyamikakārikā* when he says the following:

> Sometimes the Buddha teaches self
> Sometimes no self
> Sometimes both,
> And sometimes neither. (Garfield 1995, p. 62)

Such pedagogical versatility is what Vimalakīrti means by integrating "skill-in-means." This allows the bodhisattvas to "review" the *dharmas* without becoming attached to them, to utilize the Abhidharma analysis of experience without any commitment to their truth-value, to teach about the three "marks" of existence without treating them universally, and to preach "emptiness" while knowing full well that "it" too is "empty."

The Teaching of "Two Truths"

The Buddhist doctrine of "two truths" was developed in early Buddhism to distinguish between the "ultimate" (*paramārtha*) and "conventional" (*samvṛtti*) discourses of the Buddha. Originally, the distinction was used to help organize the extensive volumes of Buddhist literature that accumulated after the Buddha's death. The "two truths" were used to distinguish the analytic *abhidharma* texts from the discursive *sūtras*, and was simply a "convenient designation" that referred to the different ways of speaking and communicating the Dharma. Sometimes the Buddha gave precise, analytic teachings, and sometimes he told stories or offered parables. Sometimes he spoke "literally" (or "ultimately") to his disciples, and sometimes he spoke metaphorically (or "conventionally"). As the Buddhist scholar Jayatilleke (1963) notes, the difference between the "two truths" was not used epistemologically in early Buddhism, but was simply a method for understanding the various rhetorical patterns in Buddhist literature. In the later Abhidharma tradition, however, the distinction took on more weight. Instead of using it to distinguish between different ways of speaking, teaching, and communicating, the Abhidharma philosophers used it to establish normative guidelines for meditation praxis. In their view, even though the Buddha may have expressed certain "lower" or "conventional" truths to the simple-minded, he never thought these teachings had any real soteriological importance. Only those teachings contained in the *abhidharma* texts were considered "ultimately" true and, therefore, the only teachings worthy of true enlightenment.

A central aim of the *Vimalakīrtinirdeśa* is to attack the Abhidharma desire to privilege one form of religious communication above the other. In the "Skillful Means" chapter, Vimalakīrti raises the "two truths" when he teaches his neighbors about impermanence and non-self, imploring them to strive for a "higher" or "ultimate" reality:

> Friends, the body of a Tathāgata is the body of Dharma, born of gnosis. The body of a Tathāgata is born of the stores of merit and wisdom. It is born of morality, of meditation, of wisdom, of the liberations, and of the knowledge and vision of liberation . . . . It is born of the concentrations, the liberations, the meditations, and the absorptions . . . . It is born of all the transcendences . . . .

> It is born of truth. It is born of reality. It is born of conscious awareness. (Thurman 1986, p. 22)

And in a later passage, Vimalakīrti says that the Buddha relies on making a distinction between two types of truths:

> This is mundane and that is transcendental. This is compounded and that is uncompounded. This is passion and that is purification. This is life and that is liberation. (Thurman 1986, p. 82)

Nāgārjuna also uses the "two truths" in his texts, as he does here in his *Kārikās*:

> The Buddha's teaching of the Dharma
> Is based on two truths:
> A truth of worldly convention
> And an ultimate truth.
>
> Those who do not understand
> The distinction drawn between these two truths
> Do not understand
> The Buddha's profound truth. (Garfield 1995, p. 62)

We will examine Nāgārjuna's comment further in the following chapter. Important at this point is his use of a common distinction within the Mahāyāna tradition. It is also a distinction used by many Western scholars who say that Buddhism is committed to discovering a truth about existence, or that truth is necessary for liberation. One popular way is to see "conventional" truth as dealing with language and conceptual analysis. The "conventional" is the realm of the everyday, of suffering, of causal relations, of space and time, and of anything that we could possibly imagine through the use of thoughts and words. "Ultimate" truth, on the other hand, is the final goal of Buddhist insight, meditation, and practice. It transcends speech and the "mundane" world, is pure, unalloyed bliss, non-conceptual and non-dual, and beyond all categories and thought constructions. Another common way of interpreting the "two truths" is to say that the difference between the two is a matter of how we interpret the phenomenal world. The gist of the argument runs as such: what Buddhism means by "ultimate truth" is that there is no Ultimate Truth. The problems in life stem from not understanding this insight, and from taking what is merely "conventional" for something "ultimate." This is a problem because when we take things as "objective" we become attached to them, and then suffer as a result. Thus, the way to overcome this problem is to realize that what we think is ultimately "true" is in fact conditioned by culture, language, the mind, and so on.

We will return to these interpretations of the "two truths" in the following chapter. The reason for citing them now is that both share an approach to Buddhist philosophy that is rejected by the *Vimalakīrtinirdeśa*. The first claims that Buddhism is striving for an ultimate truth beyond conventions, while the second claims just the opposite. However, both share the assumption that Buddhism is committed to a fixed metaphysical system.

Vimalakīrti does not use the "two truths" in either of these ways, however. His discussion of the "two truths" is not only contained in an entire chapter devoted to "skill-in-means," but the narrative movement of Vimalakīrti's discourse from a "conventional" doctrine regarding *duḥkha* to an "ultimate truth" never veers from that topic: it is still as an *upāya* that the distinction is made. As Vimalakīrti says, the distinction between the mundane and transcendent is simply one of the "varied explanations" the Buddha uses. When the bodhisattvas ask Vimalakīrti how the Buddha teaches, for example, he responds in the following way:

> Good sirs, these living beings here are hard to discipline. Therefore, he teaches them with discourses appropriate for the disciplining of the wild and uncivilized. How does he discipline the wild and uncivilized? What discourses are appropriate? Here they are:
> "This is hell. This is the animal world. This is the world of the lord of the death. These are the adversities. These are the rebirth with crippled faculties. These are physical misdeeds, and these are the retributions for physical misdeeds . . . . This is false wisdom and this is the fruit of false wisdom . . . . This is the path and that is the wrong path. This is virtue and that is evil. This is blameworthy and that is blameless. This is defiled and that is immaculate. This is mundane and that is transcendental. This is compounded and that is uncompounded. This is passion and that is purification. This is life and that is liberation."
> Thus, by means of these varied explanations of the Dharma, the Buddha trains the minds of those living beings who are just like wild horses. Just as wild horses or wild elephants will not be tamed unless the goad pierces them to the marrow, so living beings who are wild and hard to civilize are disciplined only by means of discourses about all kinds of miseries. (Thurman 1986, p. 82)

Brief as this passage is, it expresses important ideas found throughout most Buddhist texts. It refers to the idea that life is *samsāric* and full of pain, that there are karmic retributions for certain acts, that there are compounded and uncompounded realms, and that there is such a thing called liberation. Rather than describing a true state of nature, however, Vimalakīrti says that the Buddha's reason for stating such views is to discipline unruly minds. He notes that the teaching of "two truths" is specific, directed toward the concrete problems of individuals. It is thus not metaphysical speculation—but practical advice. To teach the Dharma otherwise, as Pūrna learns from Vimalakīrti, will "wound those who are without wounds."

The above passage also implies something about the ability to overcome attachment. In attempting to "train the minds of those living beings who are just like wild horses," the Buddha is trying to get them to be less attached to their "wild" side and more focused on discipline. His way of going about this, as Vimalakīrti notes, is to teach them discourses appropriate to their needs and dispositions. The Buddha gives stories about hell realms and reincarnation, about how all things are impermanent and "empty," and stories about how "this is mundane and that is transcendental." It is obvious that they are stories and not "truths" because the sūtra tells us that they are none other than "various explanations."

In Chapter 11, it is the Buddha who says that his discourses vary depending on the audience:

> There are [discourses] that accomplish the buddha-work by means of bodhisattvas; those that do so by means of lights; those that do so by means of the tree

> of enlightenment . . . those that do so by means of religious robes . . . those that do so by means of magical incarnations; those that do so by means of empty space; and those that do so by means of lights in the sky. Why is it so, Ānanda? Because by these various means, living beings become disciplined. Similarly, Ānanda, there are [discourses] that accomplish the buddha-work by means of teaching living beings words, definitions, examples, such as 'dreams,' 'images,' . . . 'echoes,' 'illusions,' and 'mirages'; and those that accomplish the buddha-work by making words understandable. Also Ānanda, there are [discourses] that accomplish the buddha-work for living beings without speech, by silence, inexpressibility, and unteachability. Ānanda, among all the activities, enjoyments, and practices of the Buddhas, there are none that do not accomplish the buddha-work, because all discipline living beings. (Thurman 1986, p. 86)

As the Buddha suggests, all of these stories are soteriologically relevant. They embody transformative potential, and can have efficacious results if given at the right time. However, to become attached to any single story as absolutely "true" is rejected not only because it denies the concrete dispositions of individuals, but falsely assumes there is only one "correct" path (*mārga*) that suits everyone.

Vimalakīrti's complaint against those who interpret Buddhism as non-fictional "truths" is echoed in Nietzsche's complaint against those who cling to Western science as a factual system. "It is perhaps dawning on five or six minds," says Nietzsche, "that physics, too, is only an interpretation and exegesis of the world (to suit us, if I may say so!) and not a world-explanation." According to Nietzsche, the error of science is that it mistakes narrative tales for "facts," and erroneously mistakes its own narrative for something objectively "true." In his view, science is simply one story among many possible stories, and he therefore wants us to evaluate it heuristically; that is, to ask whether it paints a good narrative picture of life. In his view, science paints a loathsome view of the world, and, to counter it, Nietzsche gives an altogether different story, called the "eternal return":

> What, if some day or night a demon were to steal after you into your loneliest loneliness and say to you: "This life as you now live it and have lived it, you will have to live once more, and innumerable times more; and there will be nothing new in it, but every pain and every joy and every thought and every sigh and everything unutterably small or great in your life will have to return to you, all in the same succession and sequence—even this spider and this moonlight between the trees, and even this moment and I myself. The eternal hourglass of existence is turned upside down again and again, and you with it, speck of dust!" (*Gay Science*, trans. by Kaufmann 1974, p. 273)

In commenting on this passage, Alexander Nehamas observes that Nietzsche is not thinking of the "eternal return" as an objective "truth" about the universe. Rather, he is interested in "the attitude one must have toward oneself in order to react with joy and despair to the possibility the demon raises" (Nehamas 1985, p. 151). In other words, Nietzsche uses the idea of the eternal return as a narrative device that he thinks will transform a life based in fear and resentment to one of joy and creativity. He uses it as a catalyst. To ask whether the eternal return is true or false, or whether it depicts an accurate ontological picture of the world, not only misses the point of the story, but turns a simple narrative tale into a metaphysical problem.

The *Vimalakīrtinirdeśa* adopts a similar method for dealing with the Buddhist teachings. It tells us that "emptiness," *nirvāṇa*, impermanence, "non-self," and the "two truths" are nothing more than rhetorical strategies used within a particular discourse, and warns against the dangers of becoming attached to these teachings. The character Vimalakīrti embodies this non-attached attitude by emphasizing pedagogical versatility, audience awareness, and a spiritual resolve to help others, and by chastising those who forget the *upāyic* status of the Buddha's discourses. According to Michael Pye:

> Vimalakīrti is indeed hard to pin down. This is because every form of religious language, when conceived in terms of skilful means, is first allusive and then disposable. This applies to 'teaching Buddhism,' that is 'turning the wheel of Dharma,' and it even applies to 'entering nirvana' as observed before in *The Lotus Sutra*. In short it applies not merely to the preliminary suggestions of the religious system, but above all to its fundamental assumptions and final terms. (Pye 1978, p. 101)

Summary

It is tempting to think that Mahāyāna Buddhism signifies a complete break with early Buddhism, and that the development of "emptiness," the "two truths," the bodhisattva ideal, and *upāya* is an entirely new system of Buddhist thought. It is also tempting to think that the attack on Abhidharma Buddhism entails the rejection of all the meditation practices and religious disciplines that are found throughout the *abhidharma* texts. As we saw with Vimalakīrti, however, the issue is less about the creation of new philosophical doctrines or world-views than an attempt to restate the basic message of non-attachment. When Vimalakīrti condemns Śāriputra (a "Hīnayāna" Buddhist) for misinterpreting Buddhism, for example, he is not saying that Śāriputra has a metaphysically incorrect view of the world or that Abhidharma praxis is somehow wrong in itself. The history of Abhidharma Buddhism in Southeast Asia would certainly prove him wrong on this point. Rather, he is attacking Śāriputra on metapractical grounds, arguing that his attachment to Buddhist doctrine contradicts the message of compassion that was inaugurated by the Buddha. Thus, the issue between the Mahāyāna and the Abhidharma is not about whether the *abhidharma* texts are efficacious, or whether this or that type of meditation works, but about the philosophical justification for how one *should* meditate. In this regard, the Mahayanists argue from the perspective of *upāya*, saying there is no fixed methodology or doctrine to argue about, and that any attempt to institute a monolithic form of praxis not only violates the teachings of the Buddha, but destroys the ability to respond compassionately. In their view, the idea that one can metapractically justify a single practice for all people in all circumstances is not just anti-Buddhist and unorthodox. It is counterproductive, harmful, and ineffective.

Vimalakīrti symbolizes the opposite of the Abhidharma view because he refuses to teach others according to a fixed doctrine. Whereas someone like Śāriputra—an expert "Hīnayāna" philosopher—can recite all the categories, principles, and doctrines of Buddhist thought at will, he also assumes that the mere recitation of these "truths" will facilitate liberation. His attachment to doctrine, therefore, severs him from his audience, and he preaches without knowing anything about the thoughts and inclinations of others. Vimalakīrti, on the other hand, emphasizes intimacy and a keen awareness of the different levels of human beings. Rather than beginning with an abstract conception of Buddhist "truth" which he then teaches indiscriminately to everyone, he first begins with the concrete dispositions of others and then "teaches the Dharma appropriately to each" (Thurman 1986, p. 20). His emphasis on the "numerous teachings" and "varied explanations" underlines the fact that there are different problems depending on the individual, and makes the point that a plurality of approaches, doctrines, and teachings are necessary to address the different types of suffering that exist in the world. For this reason, says the *Vimalakīrtinirdeśa*, Vimalakīrti has fully integrated his wisdom with "skill-in-means."

Chapter 4

Nāgārjuna's Middle Way

Introduction

Nāgārjuna is widely recognized as one of the most important thinkers in the Buddhist philosophical tradition. Born in South India sometime during the second century C.E., Nāgārjuna developed a style of thinking that challenged all the major philosophical systems in India. He debated orthodox Buddhists and Hindus alike, established the "Middle Way" (Mādhyamika) school of philosophy, and refined a dialectical method (*śūnyatā* or "emptiness") that gave birth to Buddhist traditions throughout India, China, Tibet, and Japan. In many Buddhist circles, Nāgārjuna is regarded as the Second Buddha, a bodhisattva who clearly expressed the fundamentals of the "Way."

Nāgārjuna has recently become important for Western philosophers as well. Because many of his texts rely on *reductio ad absurdum* logic, and because he is seen as criticizing problems surrounding causality, subjectivity, space, and time, he is thought to be a philosopher of stature. Indeed, he is often compared to such important Western thinkers as Kant, Hegel, Hume, Wittgenstein, and Derrida, and is often situated within the same intellectual discourse as the Western tradition. According to many scholars, Nāgārjuna not only does metaphysics but also actually thinks liberation requires it. Whether he is depicted as a mystic, conventionalist, nihilist, or deconstructionist, and whether or not his dialectic of "emptiness" (*śūnyatā*) undermines all positive philosophical positions, it is commonly assumed that his philosophy addresses metaphysical problems, and that he thinks Buddhist praxis is somehow incomplete without it.

If we read Nāgārjuna as operating within an *upāyic* context, however, then this way of framing his project is misleading. The point to remember is that *upāya* has little in common with traditional Western metaphysics: it is not concerned with the nature of space and time, causality, personal identity, or consciousness, and it resists the tendency to conceptualize liberation apart from Buddhist praxis. To think otherwise assumes that the Dharma can be abstracted from its soteriological and rhetorical context, and that Buddhism can be preached without any particular audience in mind. Given the Buddhist insistence on the indispensable nature of practice, however, and given Nāgārjuna's own position within the Mahāyāna tradition, it is highly unlikely that he is raising traditional metaphysical questions, and even more unlikely that he thinks Buddhist soteriology depends on it.

The purpose of this chapter is to offer a different account of Nāgārjuna than is found in contemporary Western scholarship. It will not ask what it means for causality, truth, the self, or consciousness to be "empty" in a very general sense, but how "emptiness" relates to the soteriological practices of Buddhism and what it means for those practices to be "empty" of inherent nature.

Before examining key passages from Nāgārjuna's *Mādhyamikakārikā* that criticize Abhidharma praxis, it is important to situate Nāgārjuna within the Mahāyāna tradition. While most Buddhist scholars acknowledge Nāgārjuna's place within the Mahāyāna, many of them neglect the "skill-in-means" dimension of this tradition. The next section will therefore situate Nāgārjuna within the Mahāyāna generally, and will be followed by a "skill-in-means" reading of his *Mādhyamikakārikā*.

Nāgārjuna and Mahāyāna Buddhism

The fact that Nāgārjuna even operated within a Mahāyāna context is not obvious to some scholars. For example, A. K. Warder argues that there is very little Mahāyāna influence in Nāgārjuna's writings:

> Modern students have sometimes supposed that he is criticizing early Buddhism, or the early schools, in order to set up Mahāyāna instead. Is there any truth in this supposition? We have already pointed out that there is nothing overtly Māhāyanist in his thought. (Warder 1973, p. 13)

The problem with Warder's view is that it can easily mislead us when it comes to understanding Nāgārjuna's philosophy. In the *Twelve Gate Treatise* Nāgārjuna says that his project is based on clarifying the principles of Mahāyāna Buddhism:

> I want to reveal and make clear the supremely great teachings of the Tathāgata. Therefore, I will explain the teachings of Mahāyāna. (Cheng 1982, p. 53–54)

And in the *Bodhisaṃbhāra(ka)*, or "The Accumulations for Enlightenment," Nāgārjuna expresses views that clearly originated in the *Prajñāpāramitā* texts:

> Prajñāpāramitā is the mother of Bodhisattvas, skill-in-means is their father, and compassion is their daughter.
> Attracting with gifts, teaching the Dharma, listening to the teaching of the Dharma, and also practicing acts of benefit to others—these are the skillful means for attracting [others].
> While benefiting living beings without tiring and without carelessness, [a bodhisattva] expresses his aspiration for enlightenment: To benefit others is to benefit oneself!
> Let us not desert living beings! In order to benefit living beings, first generate this attitude and then come to possess the practice of the doors to liberation. (Lindtner 1986, p. 127)

Most Western accounts focus exclusively on the *Mādhyamikakārikā* and the *Vigrahavyāvartanī*, his most famous texts. However, Nāgārjuna's writings extend beyond these two books. He wrote for Buddhist monks, lay people, orthodox Hindus, and kings, with varying themes and philosophical motives. His writing style ranges from the simple to the complex, spanning personal devotional hymns, such as found in the *Catuḥstava*, to the more philosophically abstract, such as found in the *Kārikās*. The diversity of approaches Nāgārjuna adopts in communicating with different audiences situates him within a "skillful means" tradition that runs from the Buddha and through the Mahāyāna.

Christian Lindtner is one of the few scholars to recognize Nagarjuna's diverse literary talents, and attributes this to the notion of *upāya*:

> In my view, the decisive reasons for the variety of Nāgārjuna's writings is to be sought in the author's desire, as a Buddhist, to address himself to various audiences at various levels and from various perspectives. This motive would of course be consistent with the Mahāyāna ideal of *upāyakauśalya* (skillful means). Thus, the *Mūlamadhyamakakārikā*, the *Śūnyatāsaptati,* and *Vigrahavyāvartaī* were intended to be studied by philosophically minded monks. The *Vaidalyaprakaraṇa* was written as a challenge to Naiyayikas. The *Yuktiṣaṣṭikā*, the *Nyavaharasiddi*, and the *Pratītyasamutpādahṛdayakārikā* as well are contributions to Buddhist exegesis. The *Catuḥstava* is a document confessing its author's personal faith in the Buddha's doctrine, while texts like the *Sūtra-samuccaya*, the *Bodhicitta-vivaraṇa*, the *Bodhi-saṃbhāra(ka)*, the *Suhṛllekha*, and the *Ratnāvalī* on the whole address themselves to a wider Buddhist audience, monks as well as laymen. (Lindtner 1986, p. 331)

Lindtner groups all of Nāgārjuna's texts under the heading "skillful means." It is not just his supposed "minor" works that are geared toward a particular audience, but even those that deal with difficult concepts in Buddhist philosophy, such as the *Mādhyamikakārikā* and the *Vigrahavyāvartanī*. While no one can be sure Nagarjuna wrote all the texts ascribed to him, it is understandable why Lindtner sees Nāgārjuna as a "skill-in-means" thinker, and why he views the highly logical teaching of "emptiness" on the same footing as those given to kings, lay people, and disciples. As a Mahāyāna Buddhist, Nāgārjuna realizes that no single teaching is sufficient to cover the various "illnesses" of sentient beings, and because the world manifests itself in different degrees of karmic growth, different discourses are needed. As he says in the *Exposition of Bodhicitta*:

> The teachings of the protectors of the world accord with the [varying] resolve of living beings. The Buddhas employ a wealth of skillful means, which take many worldly forms. (Lindtner 1986, p. 65)

Nāgārjuna is saying nothing new here. It was emphasized by the Buddha, the *Lotus Sūtra*, and the *Prajñāpāramitā*, all of which emphasize the need to be sensitive to the rhetorical context of sentient beings. While Nāgārjuna rarely refers to any of these texts specifically, his devotion to this tradition is expressed through his diverse literary talents and his use of skillful means.

In the *Mādhyamikakārikā*, Nāgārjuna further aligns himself with this tradition when he says:

> That there is a self has been taught,
> And the doctrine of no-self,
> By the Buddhas, as well as the
> Doctrine of neither self nor nonself. (Garfield 1995, p. 49).

This passage suggests that the Buddha's teachings are situated within a rhetorical context, and that he relies on various teachings to liberate sentient beings. Some of these teachings include the idea that there is a self, that there is no-self, and the rejection of both alternatives. Nāgārjuna expresses a similar view when he says:

> Everything is real and is not real,
> Both real and not real,
> Neither real nor not real,
> This is the Lord Buddha's teaching. (Garfield 1995, p. 49)

Nāgārjuna's student Āryadeva was influenced by this way of thinking, as we can see from his root text, the *Catuḥśataka*:

> A student emerges for a certain [teacher], a teacher emerges for a certain [student]. A person who knows the methods [*upāyavid*] instructs ignorant living beings by various methods.
> Just as it is rare for a skilled physician not to cure patients, it is very rare for a bodhisattva who has acquired the [training] not to have [students] to be trained. (Lang 1986, p. 57)

In Chapter 6 of the same text, Āryadeva gives an example of how skill-in-means is practiced in Buddhism:

> [A student under the influence of] desire should be treated like a servant, since harshness is its antidote. [A student under the influence of] hatred should be treated like a king, since kindness is its antidote. (Lang 1986, p. 65)

Āryadeva's comments express his commitment to Nāgārjuna's style of teaching, and give voice to an entire skillful-means tradition that runs from Śākyamuni Buddha through the Mahāyāna tradition.

As a Mahāyāna Buddhist engaged in a debate with the Abhidharma Buddhists, Nāgārjuna is surely concerned with praxis and with how to communicate Buddhism to others. But what specifically divides him from the Abhidharma thinkers, and why does he think they are wrong? Do they have a false conception of reality? Are they giving a fallacious metaphysics? Most Western scholars see the Abhidharma Buddhists as concerned with traditional metaphysical issues, and see Nāgārjuna as attacking them on these grounds. According to Gudmunsen, for example, the Abhidharmists are Russellian philosophers concerned with isolating sense data and wondering how words refer to logical bits of experience (Gudmunsen 1977); for Siderits they are "epistemological realists" forging a correspondence theory of truth (Siderits 1988); for Katz they are "denotation theorists" (Katz 1981); for Garfield they are "essentialists" unwilling to accept the conventional nature of phenomena (Garfield 1995); and for Loy and Coward the Abhidharmists are proposing a metaphysical view of language (Loy 1987; Coward 1990).

When we frame Nāgārjuna's audience as concerned with these issues, however, then it means he must be dealing with them as well. That is, if the Abhidharmists are similar to the Logical Atomists, epistemological realists, metaphysicians, or philosophers of language then, since Nāgārjuna is attacking their views, he must be participating in this metaphysical discourse. But to see why this is mistaken we need to remember that the Abhidharma thinkers are specifically concerned with metapraxis, and that the general Mahāyāna critique is leveled at comments such as Vasubhandu's, when he says:

> Because there is no means of pacifying the passions without close investigation of existents, and because it is the passions that cause the world to wander in this great ocean of transmigration, therefore they say that the teacher—which means the Buddha—spoke this system aimed at the close examination of existents. For a student is not able to closely investigate existents without teaching in true doctrine. (Pruden 1988, p. 57)

The "close investigation" that Vasubandhu mentions is a precise meditation on the nature of *dharmas*, a meditation that is mindful of the impermanent, causal, and selfless nature of experience. He also implies that without meditating in a particular way (i.e., without "reviewing" the *Sarvāstivādin* analysis of *dharmas*) then it is impossible to attain liberation. In saying this, Vasubandhu is establishing the necessary conditions for practice, and, in line with traditional Abhidharma Buddhist thought, justifying a single praxis for all people.

Nāgārjuna's philosophy needs to be seen as a direct attack on this way of thinking. Like the Buddha's critique of the "sixty-two" views and Vimalakīrti's condemnation of the disciples and bodhisattvas, Nāgārjuna is trying to undermine the idea that liberation is attainable *only* upon a "close investigation" of *dharmas*. His way of doing this is to examine the meditative "matrixes" of the Abhidharma tradition—from causality and the five aggregates to impermanence, *nirvāṇa*, and the Four Noble Truths—arguing that each is "empty" of inherent nature. While it may appear that Nāgārjuna's method is excessively logical and analytic in the following discussion, we must remember that he is addressing a scholastic tradition that favors logical precision and analysis, and that he is therefore using their own way of communicating and their philosophical discourse to achieve the best rhetorical effect. The next few sections of this chapter—dealing with Nagarjuna's critique of causality, the aggregates, suffering, and the Four Noble Truths—will strive to illuminate this rhetorical style, emphasizing its *upāyic* role against the Abhidharma Buddhists.

Nāgārjuna's Critique of Causality

In the *Mādhyamikakārikā,* Nāgārjuna attacks the Abhidharma view of praxis by utilizing a system of logic that offers negative responses to four possible alternatives. Called the *catuṣkoṭi*, it is often depicted in the following form:

1. It is not the case that x is y.
2. It is not the case that x is not-y.
3. It is not the case that x is both y and not-y.
4. It is not the case that x is neither y nor not-y.

Nāgārjuna uses these four statements against a variety of arguments ranging from causality and the self to impermanence, space, time, and motion. Against a particular view of causation, for example, Nāgārjuna applies the *catuṣkoṭi* and concludes that *dharmas* (x) are not produced (y), not non-produced, neither both, nor neither. Or, against a particular view of motion he applies the dialectic and concludes that motion (x) is not moving (y), not non-moving, neither both, nor neither.

In Chapter 1 of the *Kārikās*, Nāgārjuna uses this line of reasoning against the Abhidharma views of causation:

> Neither from itself nor from another,
> Nor from both,
> Nor without a cause,
> Does anything whatever, anywhere arise.
> (Garfield 1995, p. 3)

This is the beginning of Nāgārjuna's attack on causality. Things are either caused from themselves, from something else, from both, or from no cause whatsoever. Nāgārjuna denies all four alternatives, trying to show that each view of causation is absurd.

He does this by saying that any understanding of cause and effect presupposes our ability to either affirm or deny causal identity. In other words, a cause is either identical to its effect, different from its effect, both, or neither. Saying they are identical is absurd since this destroys the language of cause and effect that tells us something has changed or has become different from what it was. If cause and effect are identical, then there is no change from the cause to the effect, which means that nothing was ever really "caused" at all. Nāgārjuna denies this alternative, saying that things cannot arise from themselves.

Does this mean that cause and effect is a relation between two different things (arising from another)? Nāgārjuna denies this alternative as well, arguing that it is logically impossible for two separate entities to be causally related. If two things are fundamentally different, then there is no connection between them whatsoever, which destroys their ability to interact causally. Just as causal identity denies the necessary relationship that must exist between causes and effects, so the idea of absolute difference ruptures any causal connection between two things that are supposedly related. According to Nāgārjuna, this idea must be rejected because it denies our ability to speak coherently about causation. "Perfect otherness (or difference)," says Candrakīrti, "amounts to no cause at all" (Sprung 1979, p. 42).

This leaves the last two alternatives, which are also denied by Nāgārjuna, the first for being contradictory, and the second for being illogical. Saying that cause and effect are both identical and non-identical is a basic contradiction: x = y and not (x = y); and saying that a cause arises from nowhere is not only logically impossible (how can a non-cause bring something into existence?), but implies that things can arise from any source whatsoever. As Buddhapālita says:

> Things cannot arise without a cause, because that would entail that anything could arise at any time, anywhere. (Sprung 1979, p. 43)

The result of Nāgārjuna's dialectic is to say that causation is "empty," without essence, inherent nature, or substance. But what does Nāgārjuna mean by saying that causation is "empty," and why is he attacking these theories in this way?

Most Western accounts say that Nāgārjuna is dealing with metaphysical problems. According to Murti (1955) and Loy (1987), for example, Nāgārjuna is arguing for a transcendental experience beyond language and conceptualization; for Siderits (1988), he is arguing against the problem of "realism"; for Kalupahana (1986) Nāgārjuna is similar to the

Logical Positivists who argue against non-empirical metaphysical views; and for Garfield (1995) Nagarjuna is arguing for the "conventional" nature of reality. These scholars also see Nagarjuna as saying that we cannot attain liberation until we fully deconstruct our metaphysical attachments. Garfield makes this clear when he writes:

> It cannot be overemphasized that as far as Nāgārjuna—or any other Mahāyāna Buddhist philosopher, for that matter—is concerned, the view that the things we perceive and of which we conceive, to the extent that they exist at all, do so inherently, originates as an innate misapprehension and is not the product of sophisticated philosophical theory. That is, we naively and pretheoretically take things as substantial. This, as Nāgārjuna will argue, and as the Buddha himself argued, is the root delusion that lies at the basis of all human suffering. (Garfield 1995, p. 88)

Garfield's generalization about all Mahāyāna Buddhist philosophers is puzzling, especially since, at least from the Mahāyāna perspective, the problem with the Abhidharma Buddhists is not their supposed metaphysical views but their attempt to justify one soteriological praxis above all others. That all Mahāyāna philosophers are concerned with metaphysics is certainly not obvious; nor it is obvious that all human suffering is caused by taking things as "substantial." Such a sweeping generalization presents a biased account of Buddhist philosophy and assumes that human suffering can be explained in a totalizing way. If Nāgārjuna is saying this, then he is guilty of offering the type of "poisonous remedies" that was rejected by the Buddha and Vimalakīrti.

If we read Nāgārjuna as a "skill-in-means" thinker, however, then we will not arrive at this conclusion. To do so, we need to remember that, like the Buddha's criticism of the "sixty two" views, Nāgārjuna is trying to resolve a major conflict in the Buddhist community over "correct" soteriological praxis. For most Abhidharma traditions, for instance, liberation depends on a "correct" meditation of *dharmas*: how they arise and cease, how they are conditioned, and how they cause suffering. While they all agreed on the need to meditate on *dharmas*, they fought over the "correct" way of going about this.

The Sarvāstivādin held that underlying the "moments" of meditation there are unchanging substances (*svabhāva*) that adhere throughout time. These underlying substances were termed a *dharma's* "self nature," and were seen as pivotal in meditative practice. To meditate on a *dharma's* "self nature" meant that one would no longer be captivated by fleeting appearances or attached to "turbulent" phenomena. One could then see the causes of suffering and mental anxiety, and rest peacefully in the "calm" of *nirvāṇa*. The ability to discern the substance of *dharmas* was therefore tantamount to liberation.

Nāgārjuna's problem with this is that it contradicts the view that one must meditate on causality in order to attain liberation. If *dharmas* stay the same then they are not caused at all because they never change; and if they are "self-caused" then they are identical to themselves, which denies the doctrine of "dependent arising." Thus, for Nāgārjuna, the Sarvāstivādin view of *dharmas* is absurd within the context of a Buddhist meditation, since the idea of *dharmas* contradicts the Buddhist doctrine of "dependent arising."

The Sautrāntikas also rejected the Sarvāstivādin position but proposed the idea that meditation is composed of continuous "flashings" of "moments" into consciousness: *dharmas* arise and cease each moment, they come from nowhere, "flash" for an instant, and then vanish. To see this process—to "review" it—was the goal of meditative practice that supposedly ends in liberation.

For Nāgārjuna, this justification of praxis suffers from similar inconsistencies as the Sarvāstivādin view. If one must meditate on *dharmas* as point-instants that have no continuity between one moment and the next, then what happens to the causal process that is vital to Buddhist praxis? If *dharmas* are nothing more than distinct "moments" in meditative equilibrium, then what is the connection between one *dharma* and the next? Since there seems to be no connection whatsoever, then how can we make sense of "dependent arising"? Nāgārjuna's point is that, like the Sarvāstivādin view, the Sautrāntikas are proposing inconsistent views of praxis: they say one must meditate on causality in order to be liberated, but then deny causality by saying that one must meditate on certain moments (*dharmas*) that are non-causal.

What is the significance of this criticism? Is Nāgārjuna saying that we should never meditate on causality, or that any meditation on *dharmas* is always wrong? Is he saying that the Abhidharma views of causation are useless because they are contradictory? It is doubtful Nāgārjuna wants us to come to this conclusion. Not only would this contradict the Buddha's own teachings about causation, it would mean that Nāgārjuna is trying to resolve the conflict between the Abhidharma traditions by renouncing Abhidharma practice altogether. However, Nāgārjuna knows that conflicts are not caused by "views," even if they are metaphysically or logically false. The problem lies much deeper than this for Nāgārjuna, and he knows that it has nothing to do with the Abhidharma view of *dharmas* or causation in itself. Like the Buddha who criticized the "sixty two" views because the philosophers who proposed them were "caught in the net" of blind grasping, Nāgārjuna could care less about the metaphysical status of *dharmas*. His concern is why the Abhidharma philosophers think there is only one type of causal meditation, and why they think there is only one way to attain liberation. By arguing for the "emptiness" of causation, he is reminding the Abhidharma Buddhists that causation, in the form of "dependent arising," is simply one of the many meditative practices taught by the Buddha, and that it is therefore nothing more than a skillful "device" used to counter certain forms of attachment. Rather than arguing against a metaphysical view of causation, he is simply recalling the Buddha's own words on the subject: "If you cling to it, if you fondle it, if you treasure it, if you are attached to it, then you do not understand that the teaching is similar to a raft, which is for crossing over, and not for getting hold of" (Rahula 1974, p. 11).

The Five Aggregates

In Chapter 4 of the *Kārikās*, Nāgārjuna continues his criticism of the Abhidharma tradition by examining the "five aggregates" (or *skandhas*), which, like causality, is central to Buddhist meditation. Beginning with the first aggregate, form (*rūpa*), Nāgārjuna applies his *reductios* against the idea that either form or the cause of form must exist in a substantial way:

Apart from the cause of form,
Form cannot be conceived.
Apart from form,
The cause of form is not seen.

If apart from the cause of form, there were form,
Form would be without cause.
But nowhere is there an effect
Without a cause.

If apart from form,
There were a cause of form,
It would be a cause without an effect.
But there are no causes without effects.
(Garfield 1995, p. 48)

In these lines, Nāgārjuna argues against the idea that the *rūpa* aggregate exists essentially or contains a *svabhāva* ("self nature"). If we keep in mind the Abhidharma view that a *dharma's* "self nature" is wound up with an explanation of causality, we will understand what Nāgārjuna is up to in these passages. The Abhidharma positions rest on the idea that a *dharma* is either different from or identical to its causal properties, and Nāgārjuna is trying to show how both views lead to absurd conclusions.

If the Sautrāntikas are right in saying that a thing is essentially different from its cause, then we should be able to speak of cause and effect as two separate things. On the other hand, if the Sarvāstivādin are right in saying that a *dharma* is identical to its causal relations, then we should not be able to distinguish a cause from its effect since they are numerically the same. What Nāgārjuna says about both positions is contained in the above verses. It makes no sense, he says, to separate the aggregate *rūpa* from its cause because we then have the conclusion that *rūpa* can exist without any causal relations whatsoever, i.e., that cause and effect are two separate "things." This means that an effect can exist without a cause, and that a cause can exist without an effect. But this conclusion is absurd, says Nāgārjuna, since nowhere do we find causes without effects, or effects without causes. The two terms stand in a relation, thus making it logically impossible to assert their independence.

In the next three verses, Nāgārjuna continues his critique by saying that if *rūpa* has an identifiable essence, something that could be classified as *svabhāva*, then it makes no sense to speak of something else "causing" it to arise since it already exists as an independent entity. Similarly, a non-existent cause for *rūpa* is logically incoherent, since if it is non-existent then it makes no sense to claim that it could cause other things to arise:

> When form exists,
> A cause of the arising of form is not tenable.
> When form is non-existent,
> A cause of the arising of form is not tenable.
>
> Form itself without a cause
> Is not possible or tenable.
> Therefore, think about form, but
> Do not construct theories about form.
>
> The assertion that the effect and cause are similar
> Is not acceptable.

The assertion that they are not similar
Is also not acceptable. (Garfield 1995, p. 49)

The Sarvāstivādin position was already shown to lead to absurdity, and is therefore quickly dismissed in the above sections. If cause and effect are identical then it makes no sense to speak about causation since causation implies that there is some amount of change that occurs between things. The conclusion, as Nāgārjuna asserts in verse six, is that an essential effect is neither different from nor similar to an essential cause, since the whole idea of something having an essence, either a "self nature" or an "other nature," is absurd:

The assertion that the effect and cause are similar
Is not acceptable.
The assertion that they are not similar
Is also not acceptable. (Garfield 1995, p. 49)

Note that Nāgārjuna does not propose another correct view of "form" over and above the Abhidharma traditions. He simply argues against their views by showing how their discussion is incoherent, and rather than propose another view he simply says to "think about form" but not to get attached to it:

Therefore, think about form, but
Do not construct theories about form. (Garfield 1995, p. 50)

In other words, meditate on the body, the sense organs, and experiences of taste, smells, sensations, and sounds, but do not construct metapractical justifications for these meditative experiences. This conclusion is then extended to all the other aggregates as well:

> Feelings, discrimination and dispositions
> And consciousness and all such things
> Should be thought of
> In the same way as material form. (Garfield 1995, p. 50)

The majority of arguments in the *Kārikās* proceed along these lines. The idea of *svabhāva*, essence, substance, or inherent nature is attacked for being inconsistent, which makes the Abhidharma insistence on needing to meditate in a particular way utterly foolish. From an analysis of causality and the aggregates, Nāgārjuna moves on to the other major factors in Abhidharma analysis of experience, performing the same task in each case: deconstructing the view of *svabhāva* without putting another definitive view of praxis in its place.

Suffering, Attachment, and Bondage

In the chapter "Examination of Suffering," Nāgārjuna argues against the view that suffering can be explained in an essentialistic way. This is an important chapter of the *Kārikās* because it goes against the prevailing view in Indian philosophy that suffering needs to be an object of meditative praxis, i.e., that we must meditate on the nature of suffering and how it arises in order to achieve liberation. Nāgārjuna begins by laying out four popular theories on how suffering arises:

Some say suffering is self-produced,
Or produced from another or from both.
Or that it arises without a cause.
It is not the kind of thing to be produced.
(Garfield 1995, p. 33)

Nāgārjuna ends the verse by stating the conclusion: Suffering is not the kind of thing that can be explained by appealing to some form of inherent production. He then goes on to explain that suffering is not self-produced because that would entail speaking of production in isolation from causal conditions, i.e., production without any real cause and effect. It cannot come from something wholly other because the idea of essential difference precludes the necessary relationship that must adhere between conditioned things. The final two alternatives are rejected for leading to similar conclusions: To say that suffering is both self-produced and other-produced is a basic contradiction, and saying that it arises without any cause whatsoever implies that things can arise from nowhere, which make little sense. Nāgārjuna concludes the chapter by criticizing an essentialistic view of suffering:

Not only does suffering not exist
In any of the fourfold ways:
No external entity exists
In any of the fourfold ways. (Garfield 1995, p. 34)

Nowhere in this chapter does Nāgārjuna say what suffering is in itself. He offers no new theory on how it comes about, what its nature is, or what we need to know in order to achieve liberation. His goal is simply to refute those theories that rely on an essentialistic understanding of suffering. Not only does suffering lack an essence (at least in the way the Abhidharma thinkers think of it), but it is absurd to speak of "external entities" as existing in this way as well. By attacking the idea that suffering has an essence, he is trying to undermine the view that suffering must be an object of meditative praxis.

Nāgārjuna's critique of essentialism in regards to suffering is also applied to the causes of suffering. According to a number of Indian philosophies, one needs to meditate on the causes of suffering in order to overcome it, and most traditions agreed that suffering, *saṁsāra*, bondage, and disease are caused by attachment, either to the fruits of action, the *guṇas, Prakṛti*, an empirical "self," friends, relatives, or material things. Nāgārjuna also shares this view, but ascribes no significance to the idea that attachment must be an object of meditative praxis. Just as causality, *rūpa*, and suffering are "empty," then so too is attachment—without essence, substance, or inherent nature.

This idea is developed in the "Examination of Bondage" chapter, in which Nāgārjuna argues against the idea that the essence of *saṁsāra* can be located in the act of "grasping." The gist of the argument is that if grasping (attachment) has an inherent nature then we should be able to identify the subject of attachment, the "grasper." In other words, if there is "grasping" then there must be some essential subject that actually does the grasping. But since no essential subject can be found, according to Nāgārjuna, it follows that the idea of an essential "grasping" is impossible.

> If grasping were bondage,
> Then the one who is grasping would not be bound.

But one who is not grasping is not bound.
In what circumstances will one be bound?

If prior to binding
There is a bound one,
There would be bondage, but there isn't.
The rest has been explained by the gone, the not-gone, and the goer. (Garfield 1995, p.41)

Nāgārjuna's goal here is to drive a wedge between bondage and the person bound. If bondage does have an essence, then, like all essences, it must exist as an independent phenomenon, separate from and prior to the person becoming bound. Similarly, if a person has an essence, a *svabhāva*, then it too must be separate from the act of grasping that is identified as bondage. What Nāgārjuna says above, however, is that this creates an untenable dualism. If the person "grasping" has an inherent nature independent from that act, then it is obviously not bound, and if it is not bound, then the whole idea of needing to get out of bondage makes no sense. The separation between the subject which grasps, the act of grasping, and the experience of being bound--all three of which are needed to identify an essential "grasping"—is a separation that excludes the necessary relationship that must adhere between these activities. It is like severing the relation between motion and moving, which, as Nāgārjuna explains in Chapter 2 of the *Kārikās*, leads to the absurd conclusion that there is no movement.

The reification of suffering, attachment, and bondage that Nāgārjuna criticizes here goes hand in hand with a reification of non-attachment, or *nirvāṇa,* as well. When *saṁsāra* is essentialized into a fixed principle with its own "inherent nature"—then *nirvāṇa* is separated off, distinguished from all other things, and reified into a realm of independence. Such a radical separation severs any possible relationship between being bound and achieving liberation, and leads to the conclusion that whatever is bound must necessarily remain bound, and whatever is released must stay released. As Nāgārjuna puts it:

> Whoever is bound is not released.
> Whoever is not bound does not get released. (Garfield 1995, p. 42)

This is an unacceptable conclusion for Nagarjuna—or any other Indian philosopher who values liberation—and is why Nāgārjuna ends the chapter with the following question:

> When you can't bring about nirvāṇa,
> Nor the purification of cyclic existence,
> What is cyclic existence,
> And what is the nirvāṇa you examine? (Garfield 1995, p. 42)

Nāgārjuna's point here is to say that liberation is impossible if *saṁsāra* and *nirvāṇa* are substantially existent things. To think of grasping, bondage, suffering, and liberation as distinct objects of meditative praxis treats them as fixed and static entities, which severs any possible relationship between them. If this happens, then something bound can never become unbound, and someone who suffers can never hope for release. Since this is an unacceptable conclusion for any Buddhist, then the problem lies in the way liberation is being conceived.

In moving from causality, the aggregates, and the elements of existence to suffering, attachment, *saṁsāra,* and *nirvāṇa*, Nāgārjuna has covered the major areas of Buddhist practice. In each case he undermines the idea of *svabhāva*—thus undermining the assumption that these terms, categories, and experiences are necessary for liberation. If there is no essence to causality, to suffering, to attachment, or to *nirvāṇa*, then they are, as Nāgārjuna says, "empty" of inherent nature; and if they are "empty," then the Abhidharma view that one *must* meditate on them is unwarranted.

This does not mean that one should never meditate on causality, the *dharmas*, *skandhas*, or *saṁsāra* as elements of experience, or that there is anything inherently wrong with the *abhidharma* texts themselves. Nāgārjuna is not arguing against the meditative practices of these texts, but against the philosophical justifications of the Abhidharma philosophers who are justifying these texts as the *only* soteriological "rafts" in Buddhism.

In this sense, Nāgārjuna, along with the *Lotus Sūtra,* the *Prajñāpāramitā*, and *Vimalakīrtinirdeśa*, takes a strong philosophical stance: there are no fixed or absolute metapractical criteria in Buddhism, and the attempt to justify any single practice for all people under all circumstances not only contradicts Buddhist doctrine, but goes against the spirit of compassion that meditative praxis is trying to facilitate. While this may look like simply one more "view" among all the others, it is not a metapractical—or metaphysical—"view" that seeks to totalize Buddhist praxis under a single heading. In this respect, Nāgārjuna has no "view."

Nāgārjuna's Critique of the Four Noble Truths

Chapter 24 of the *Kārikās* contains some of the most important sections of the entire text, and begins with an obvious rejoinder to everything Nāgārjuna has argued against up to this point. If it is true, as Nāgārjuna says, that causality, impermanence, suffering, bondage, and so on are all "empty," then what is left of Buddhism? In other words, if it is true that the Abhidharma justifications of practice are "empty," and if it is true that their views of praxis are central to Buddhist meditation and doctrine, then Nāgārjuna seems to be undermining everything that is vital to Buddhism. He begins Chapter 24 by expressing this complaint in the following way:

> If all of this is empty,
> Neither arising nor ceasing,
> Then for you, it follows that
> The Four Noble Truths do not exist.
>
> If the Four Noble Truths do not exist,
> Then knowledge, abandonment,
> Meditation and manifestation
> Will be completely impossible.
>
> If these things do not exist,
> The four fruits will not arise.
> Without the four fruits, there will be no attainers of the fruits.
> Nor will there be the faithful.

> If so, the spiritual community will not exist.
> Nor will the eight kinds of person.
> If the Four Noble Truths do not exist,
> There will be no true Dharma.
>
> If there is no doctrine and spiritual community,
> How can there be a Buddha?
> If emptiness is conceived in this way,
> The three jewels are contradicted. (Garfield 1995, p. 67)

In the above passages, the Abhidharma opponent argues that if Nāgārjuna is right about "emptiness," then the very practices that make Buddhism soteriologically efficacious will be destroyed. That is, if it is true that the Four Noble Truths are "empty," then there is no such thing as the Buddha, the Dharma, and the Sangha, no such thing as impermanence, "non-self," and *nirvāṇa*, and the practices that supposedly lead to liberation will be destroyed. Nāgārjuna responds to this complaint by saying it relies on a misinterpretation of *śūnyatā*:

> We say that this understanding of yours
> Of emptiness and the purpose of emptiness
> And of the significance of emptiness is incorrect.
> As a consequence you are harmed by it.
> (Garfield 1995, p. 68)

Because the Abhidharma opponent takes "emptiness" to mean the non-existence of the Four Noble Truths, he is "harmed by it," in other words, he sees "emptiness" as destroying Buddhist praxis altogether. But his reason for thinking like this is because he thinks that practice requires fixed metapractical criteria.

Nāgārjuna responds to this assumption by reversing the tables, saying that what destroys practice is not "emptiness," but rather the idea that there must be an essential practice (*svabhāva)* that applies to everyone universally:

> If you perceive the existence of all things
> In terms of [*svabhāva]*,
> Then this perception of all things
> Will be without the perception of causes and conditions.
>
> Effects and causes
> And agent and action
> And conditions and arising and ceasing
> And effects will be rendered impossible.
> Garfield 1995, p. 69)

Nāgārjuna goes on to say that the reason *svabhāva* militates against causal conditions, arising, ceasing, agency, and so forth, is because *svabhāva* entails independence, and if things are independent then it is impossible for them to interact causally. If this is true then there is no "dependent arising," and without "dependent arising" it is impossible to make sense of the ability to cultivate a virtuous life. In other words, without the process of change the whole idea of cultivating the "fruits" of a Buddhist life is rendered nonsensical. In short, he says that Buddhist praxis must be "empty" if we are to make any sense of the Four Noble Truths:

> If dependent arising is denied,
> Emptiness itself is rejected.

This would contradict
All of the worldly conventions.

If emptiness is rejected,
No action will be appropriate.
There would be action which did not begin,
And there would be agent without action.

If there is [*svabhāva*], the whole world
Will be unarising, unceasing,
And static. The entire phenomenal world
Would be immutable.

If it (the world) were not empty,
Then action would be without profit.
The act of ending suffering and
Abandoning misery and defilement would not exist.
(Garfield 1995, p. 72)

Nāgārjuna has thus shifted the debate. Whereas the Abhidharma thinker began with the assumption that fixed metapractical criteria are necessary for liberation, Nāgārjuna counters by saying that Buddhist practice—and hence liberation—is undermined by treating it as a fixed system. Like the first chapter on causation, Nāgārjuna is attacking the Abhidharma Buddhists for their attachment to meditation and for thinking that one can reduce Buddhism to an absolute soteriological guide. The Four Noble Truths are supposed to be medicinal "rafts" that help particular human beings overcome attachment, but if one becomes attached to those practices of non-attachment then the entire thrust of Buddhism is lost. Thus, Nāgārjuna says that the

Dharma—which includes causation, impermanence, suffering, bondage, and liberation—must remain "empty."

Summary

During Nāgārjuna's time there were prolific debates over issues such as the nature of personal identity, the mind, consciousness, the status of knowledge, causality, and the structure of experience. While it is possible to discuss these debates in purely metaphysical terms and apart from their South Asian milieu, we need to remember that these debates take place within a soteriological context and are linked to issues of praxis. The debates over causality in the Buddhist tradition, for example, are not about knowing how the world is structured or getting an objective view on causation, but about how a meditation on *dharmas* allows us to overcome the causes of suffering, attachment, and bondage. Likewise, the debates over the "means of knowledge" (*pramāṇa*) between the Nyāya and Buddhist philosophers has little to do with the epistemological problem of how we know, or how we know that we know, but is about the role of knowledge and cognition in meditative praxis. Thus, while it might be interesting to examine these issues apart from how they operate in a metapractical discourse, and while we could discuss them in relation to general metaphysical, ontological, or epistemological problems, we end up distorting the issue if we frame these debates apart from their metapractical context and apart from how they relate to issues of mediation, practice, and soteriology.

It is nevertheless common to confuse Nāgārjuna's metapractical critique—dealing with attachment to Buddhist praxis—with metaphysics because it appears that the Abhidharma philosophers are giving a metaphysical justification for their views. As was discussed in Chapter 2, however, it is doubtful that the conflict between the Abhidharma traditions can be framed in this way since their views are inseparably linked to praxis: they are not offering theories of causality in the abstract—but metapractical justifications of how one *should* meditate. Nāgārjuna's philosophy challenges such justifications, arguing for the "emptiness" of causality, the *dharmas*, *skandhas*, the Four Noble Truths, and suffering. And instead of justifying "emptiness" as a new fixed meditative standard for all Buddhists, Nāgārjuna argues that even "emptiness" is "empty." In saying this, he not only undermines the Abhidharma fixation with a specific form of praxis—those found in the *abhidharma* texts—but tries to undermine our own desire to become attached to "emptiness." While this may presuppose certain assumptions about the nature of the world and human beings, it does not entail a metapractical justification for any single meditative practice. And it is in this sense that we should understand Nagarjuna's claim that he has no fixed "view" (*dṛṣṭi*).

The divisions between the two Mādhyamika schools that followed Nāgārjuna, the Prāsaṅgika and Svatāntrika, are separated by similar issues of praxis, and therefore immersed in a skillful-means debate. The issue that separates them is about the best way to communicate "emptiness" to other Buddhist and non-Buddhist schools in India. The Svatāntrika philosopher Bhāvaviveka, for example, thought the best way to express "emptiness" is to use arguments that conform to accepted modes of argumentation. By relying on an independent syllogism (*svatantra-anumāna*), he felt that the Mādhyamikan philosopher would be more effective in inducing an understanding of "emptiness" to others because he would then use inferential norms accepted by both parties. According to Candrakīrti, however, the Mādhyamika system begins only with views and assertions of other people and does not rely on an independent inference. It admits only provisionally the argument of the opponent and then shows, through *reductio ad absurdum* (*prasaṅga*) arguments, the untenability of the position being advanced. As Peter Della Santina notes, the issue for the Prāsaṅghika is not whether an argument is true inferentially but whether it will work soteriologically:

> They have as their paradigm the conduct of the Enlightened Ones who by means of appropriate arguments edify the ignorant. In such a context, the validity of an argument is measured by its efficacy, not by its conformity to the principles of formal logic and epistemology. (Della Santina 1986, p. 69)

From a metapractical perspective, the debate between the two Mādhyamika schools is a debate about the nature and efficacy of the Buddhist system, and has little to do with strictly metaphysical or logical issues. Nāgārjuna's debate with the Abhidharma philosophers should be seen in a similar light: he is not asking how causation is possible at all, or which philosophical theory is most feasible, but why the Abhidharma thinkers are justifying this particular view of praxis, and why they think it represents the highest soteriological wisdom of the Buddha.

Chapter 5

Ch'an Buddhism

Introduction

The Ch'an (Japanese Zen) Buddhist tradition offers some of the most exciting and interesting uses of *upāya*. Although developed first in China and then later in Japan, Ch'an has its roots in India, and claims to preserve the pedagogical styles and teachings of the Buddha. Two obvious examples of "skill-in-means" in Ch'an include the use of *kung-an* (Japanese *koan*), that are used to initiate a spiritual awakening in a student, and Ch'an meditation (Japanese *zazen*), that resembles the traditional Buddhist practice of "mindfulness." In many Ch'an schools, the doctrine of *upāya* is extended to include the devotional elements of Pure Land Buddhism such that faith in Amida Buddha will itself lead one to the Pure Land. This reliance on "other power" (Chinese *t'o-li*; Japanese *tariki*) in which a practitioner can simply invoke the name of Amida Buddha (*nien-fo*) to attain enlightenment is considered a valid path in some Ch'an traditions, and is said to have originally been taught by the Buddha himself.

The Ch'an use of *upāya* is particularly interesting because it highlights the critical element of non-attachment. As we have seen, *upāya* counteracts the tendency to reify any one teaching, doctrine, or practice by saying that all the Buddha's teachings are rhetorically efficacious: they suit the different levels and karmic dispositions of an audience. Hence, the use of paradoxical *kung-ans*, *ch'an* meditation *(dhyāna)*, and "other power" devotion are fully compatible and syncretic doctrines, and make perfect sense within the pedagogical context of skillful means. However, Ch'an is also sensitive to the long-standing problem of essentializing Buddhist practice and the problem of saying that only one of these practices will lead to liberation. While this struggle against Buddhist attachment is by no means unique to the Ch'an tradition, it did develop an iconoclastic resistance to attachment by exclaiming, as Lin-chi did, that there is no Buddhist doctrine whatsoever, no such thing as enlightenment, and that the scriptures are nothing more than "old toilet paper to wipe away excrement." Such extreme statements—which can also include a slap, kick, or punch by a Ch'an master—take place within a larger debate about Buddhist practice and need to be seen as strategic maneuvers within the context of *upāya*.

This chapter is therefore not about the Ch'an tradition per se, although it will obviously be the main focus of the following discussion. Rather, this chapter, like all the preceding chapters, is about exploring an on-going critical dialogue within the Buddhist tradition, a dialogue that began with the Buddha's critical stance toward his own teachings, re-emerged in the *Prajñāpāramitā* texts, the *Vimalakīrti*, and Nāgārjuna, and is seen again in the Ch'an tradition. It is therefore not about Ch'an metaphysics, non-duality, language, enlightenment, or the doctrine of "No-Mind," but about a larger debate over Buddhist praxis. As the Japanese Ch'an master Dōgen says:

> You should know that in the buddha's house we do not discuss superiority or inferiority of the teaching; nor do we concern ourselves with the depth or shallowness of

the dharma, but only with the genuineness or falseness of practice. (Tanahashi 1985, p. 149)

The following section will examine this issue of practice by looking briefly at key representatives of the Ch'an tradition, such as Hui-neng, Lin-chi, and Dōgen. It will end with some concluding remarks about the harmonious relationship between Ch'an and Pure Land.

Shen-hsiu and Hui-neng

The problem of Buddhist praxis is contained in a famous struggle between Shen-hsiu and Hui-neng over who will become the Sixth Patriarch of Ch'an Buddhism. The Fifth patriarch, Hung-jen, had grown old and needed to choose a successor to pass the "robe" of patriarchal authority, an established tradition in Ch'an since the Buddha first passed it to Mahākāshyapa. One day the Fifth Patriarch gathered his disciples before him and said that the monk who writes the best poem (*gāthā)* will receive the robe. The next day, a monk named Shen-hsiu, famous for his intellect and unwavering commitment to practice, offered the following *gāthā* to the Fifth Patriarch:

The body is the Bodhi tree,
The mind is like a clear mirror.
At all times we must strive to polish it,
And must not let the dust collect.

Shen-hsiu's *gāthā* expresses a fundamental point in Buddhism: the importance of practice. The first line compares the body to the tree of wisdom under which the Buddha sat, and implies that it is a vital ingredient in all meditation praxis, and, hence, enlightenment itself. The second line compares the mind to a mirror that, when clear, can reflect all things as they truly are. However, the mind of ordinary people is not like this, and they must continually "polish" it in order to reach enlightenment. As Shen-hsiu implies in the third and fourth lines, the way to clear the mind of dust is by continual, vigilant practice. Through meditation, the mind will purify itself of attachments and reveal the reflective brilliance of enlightenment.

According to the *Platform Sūtra*, however, Shen-hsiu did not receive the robe from the Fifth Patriarch. Rather, it was given to an uneducated kitchen-hand named Hui-neng, who composed his own *gāthā* for the Patriarch:

> Originally there is no tree of enlightenment,
> Nor is there a stand with a clear mirror.
> From the beginning not one thing exists;
> Where, then, is a grain of dust to cling?

Hui-neng's *gāthā* is diametrically opposed to Shen-hsiu's. It rejects the idea that the body is a "tree" of wisdom, that the mind is like a mirror, and that there is any place for dust to collect. Where Shen-hsiu affirms the body as the basis of meditation practice, Hui-neng says there is no body, and where Shen-hsiu expresses the importance of purifying one's mind, Hui-neng rejects the mind. Given that Hui-neng seems to be rejecting the very basis of enlightenment and practice, why did he receive the robe?

To understand the issue that Hui-neng's *gāthā* raises we need to see it in relation to a long critical tradition of

Buddhism. Like Nāgārjuna's attack against the Abhidharma tradition and Vimalakīrti's anger at the Buddha's immediate disciples, Hui-neng is trying to undermine Shen-hsiu's traditional stance that enlightenment only comes about by following a specific practice of meditation. He rejects the bodily postures and "polishing" mind that was also standard practice in Abhidharma Buddhism, and tries to undermine the essentialist attitude toward practice that Shen-hsiu's "dusting" metaphor implies.

A similar point is made by Ma-tsu when he observes another Ch'an master in meditation:

> He [Ma-tsu] was residing in the monastery of Dembo-in where he sat constantly in meditation. The master, aware that he was a vessel of the Dharma, went to him and asked, "Virtuous one, for what purpose are you sitting in meditation?"
>
> Tao-I answered, "I wish to become a Buddha."
>
> Thereupon the master picked up a tile and started rubbing it on a stone in front of the hermitage.
>
> Tao-I asked, "What is the Master doing?"
>
> The master replied, "I am polishing [this tile] to make a mirror."
>
> "How can you make a mirror by polishing a tile?" exclaimed Tao-i.
>
> "And how can you make a Buddha by practicing *ch'an*?" countered the master. (Dumoulin 1988, p.163)

It is tempting to think that Ma-tsu and Hui-neng are attacking the epistemological assumptions of these other Buddhists. Both Shen-shui and Tao-I compare the mind to a mirror, and say that through continual practice one can attain enlightenment. By speaking of the mind as something distinct from its experiences (or the mirror from its dust) they seem to be erecting fallacious epistemological and metaphysical distinctions. A number of Ch'an scholars tend to frame the problem in this manner, seeing the problem as a dualistic view of the mind. As Steven Laycock put it:

> Only by overcoming the conflictual duality of meditational *practice* and the profound "seeing" that is "theory" (*theoria*) in a sense akin to that which this term held for the Greeks, could the transaction of ordinary life (*saṁsāra*) be rendered consistent with the attainment of supreme insight (*nirvāṇa*). (Laycock 1994, p. 5)

Laycock sees the issue between Hui-neng and Shen-hsiu as an epistemological problem related to the idea of a mind that mirrors the world. Like Richard Rorty's criticism of Western philosophy (Rorty 1980), he sees Hui-neng trying to overcome a subject/object dualism in Shen-hsiu's view of the mind, and says that only by overcoming this "conflictual duality" can liberation be achieved.

While there is nothing wrong in viewing Ch'an as a critical response to epistemological problems, it departs from the issue of practice that is central to Hui-neng and Shen-hsiu. The issue that divides them is whether there is any single practice that leads to enlightenment, and whether the Buddha originally taught this practice. Shen-hsiu thinks there is, and assumes that enlightenment comes about through a continual "polishing" of the mind. He not only separates meditation from enlightenment but thinks that it is impossible to attain enlightenment without "polishing" in a particular way. Hui-neng attacks this view of meditation and promotes a "sudden" awakening that relies on no pre-established methodological procedure or fixed practice. In his view, there is no causal relationship between meditating and attaining enlightenment since liberation is a direct and unmediated encounter, or, in the words of Bodhidharma, "a direct pointing to the mind of man."

Thus, the differences between Hui-neng and Shen-hsiu are not so much metaphysical or epistemological as they are methodological. That is, Hui-neng is not criticizing Shen-hsiu because Shen-hsiu has a dualistic view of consciousness, or because his *gāthā* implies an erroneous view of the mind, or even because Shen-hsiu tends to substantialize the nature of "dust." Rather, Hui-neng's criticism is leveled at the methodological prescriptions involved in Shen-hsiu's account of Buddhist praxis.

Shen-hsiu's approach to praxis—which can be found in any number of Buddhist texts from the Buddha's *Satipaṭṭhāna Sutta* to Buddhaghosa's *Visuddhi-magga*—focuses almost exclusively on meditation techniques; on bodily posture, breathing, concentration, awareness of physiological sensations, observation, and so forth, and emphasizes the need to cultivate insight (*vipaśyanā*) into our emotional and mental lives. Dōgen's advice to his monks on how to practice "just sitting" (Japanese *zazen*) brings out the flavor in this approach:

> Loosen your robes and arrange them in an orderly way. Place the right hand on the left foot and the left hand on the right hand, lightly touching the ends of the thumbs together. With the hands in this position, place them next to the body so that the joined thumb-tips are at the navel.

> Straighten your body and sit erect. Do not lean to the left or right; do not bend forward or backward. Your ears should be in line with your shoulders, and your nose in line with your navel.
>
> Rest your tongue against the roof of your mouth, and breathe through your nose. Lips and teeth should be closed. Eyes should be open, neither too wide, nor too narrow. Having adjusted body and mind in this manner, take a breath and exhale fully.
>
> Sit solidly in *samādhi* and think not-thinking. How do you think not thinking? Nonthinking. This is the art of *zazen*. (Tanahashi 1985, p. 30)

By focusing on meditation practice, the "gradual" approach highlights the Buddhist concern for "cultivating the path," achieving mindfulness, and the appropriate methods for overcoming mental anguish, suffering, and spiritual distress, i.e., *saṁsāra*. In this sense, Shen-hsiu expresses what Conze calls "the very core of the Buddhist approach to life" (Conze 1956, p. 11), and situates himself within a meditative tradition that dates back to Śākyamuni Buddha.

As Peter Gregory notes, the "Sixth Patriarch's criticism of the formal practice of meditation in the *Platform Sūtra* only makes sense within the context of the daily regimen of the Ch'an or Zen monk, where seated meditation is an integral part of his practice, if not the major focus of his life" (Gregory 1986, p. 3). It is therefore doubtful that Hui-neng has a problem with meditation itself, or thinks that "polishing" is completely ineffectual. On the other hand, what disturbs Hui-neng is that Shen-hsiu seems to focus exclusively on *how* to attain enlightenment rather than enlightenment itself, and therefore reduces all of Buddhism to a fixed methodology. The seventeenth-century Japanese master Bankei expresses a similar point when he says:

> Zen masters of today generally use "old tools" when they deal with pupils, apparently thinking they cannot raise the barriers [to enlightenment] without them. They do not teach by thrusting themselves directly forward and confronting their students without their tools. These men who teach with tools and cannot do without them are blind men of Zen. (Waddell 1973, p, 147)

Like Vimalakīrti who scolds Śāriputra for his dogmatic attachment to a particular form of meditation, Hui-neng is attacking Shen-hsiu for mistaking "meditation" for ritualized behavior, and for restricting enlightenment to a select few, in other words, to those who can engage in lengthy years of practice. Hui-neng's teachings, on the other hand, are supposedly open to everyone such that even "illiterate barbarians" (like Hui-neng) can attain enlightenment.

While the differences between Hui-neng and Shen-hsiu later divided into the Southern and Northern schools, each vying for orthodoxy and claiming to be in possession of "true" Buddhist praxis, many Ch'an masters see no conflict whatsoever between them. The Japanese Ch'an master Dōgen makes this point in his discussion of Bodhidharma's transmission to Hui-k'o ("Huike"):

> The Twenty-eighth Ancestor [Bodhidharma] once said to his students, "The time has come. Can you express your understanding?"
>
> Then one of the students, Daofu, said, "My present view is that we should neither be attached to letters nor

> be apart from letters, and allow the way to function freely."
>
> The ancestor said, "You have attained my skin."
>
> The nun Zongchi said, "My view is that it is like the joy of seeing Akshobhya Buddha's land just once and not again."
>
> The ancestor said, "You have attained my flesh."
>
> Daoyu said, "The four great elements are originally empty and the five skandhas do not exist. Therefore I see nothing to be attained."
>
> The ancestor said, "You have attained my bones."
>
> Finally Huike answered by bowing three times, stood up, and returned to where he was.
>
> The Ancestor said, "You have attained my marrow." Thus he confirmed Huike as the Second Ancestor and transmitted to him dharma and robe. (Tanahashi 1985, p. 169)

It is tempting to think that Hui-k'o's response is the correct answer since, like Hui-neng, he was given the robe. However, Dōgen resists this temptation by telling us that all the students' answers are "correct":

> You should not see or hear the ancestor with a limited understanding of these statements. Otherwise, what was spoken and heard will not be fully grasped. However, those who have not yet received correct transmission think that the ancestor's words "skin, flesh, bones, and marrow" are not equal in shallowness and depth, and because the views of the four students vary, one may seem to be closer than the others. They think that skin and flesh are not as close as bones and marrow.

> They think that the Second Ancestor was acknowledged as attaining the marrow because his view was better than those of the others. [But] you should know that the ancestor's words "skin, flesh, bones, and marrow" do not mean that one understanding is closer than another . . . . It means that neither the phrase "You have attained my marrow" nor the phrase "You have attained my bones" is more essential than the other for guiding a person in holding up grass, dropping grass. It is like holding up a flower, or it is like transmitting a robe. From the beginning, Bodhidharma's confirmation of each was equal. (Tanahashi 1985, p. 170)

The phrase "holding up grass, dropping grass," and the phrase "holding up a flower" are metaphors for enlightenment. When Śākyamuni Buddha held up an udumbara flower and winked in the midst of a vast assembly, there was only one disciple (Mahākāshyapa) who fully understood its significance. However, this does not mean that "holding up a flower" is the *only* way to express enlightenment or guide a person in "holding up grass, dropping grass." As Dōgen says, Bodhidharma is not privileging one view above all the others, and is not saying that "attaining the marrow" is more essential than "attaining the flesh." While the views obviously differ—i.e., the view of non-attachment ("attaining the skin") is not the same as Hui-k'o's silent bow ("attaining the marrow")—they are nonetheless equal since they all express a soteriological experience between Bodhidharma and his students. If Bodhidharma had hundreds or thousands of students, says Dōgen, "he would have spoken hundreds or thousands of words. There should be no limit. Because he had only four students he spoke of 'skin, flesh, bones, and marrow.'

But the words not spoken, and yet to be spoken, should be many" (Tanahashi 1986, p. 170).

Following Dōgen's analysis, we can say that Shen-hsiu's problem has nothing to do with metaphysics or epistemology since his view is just as "true" as Hui-neng's in "holding up grass, dropping grass." The seated "mind-polishing" meditation of Shen-shiu is no less essential than Hui-neng's "sudden" approach, just as Nāgārjuna's "emptiness" is no "truer" than the Abhidharma philosophy of *svabhāva*. The problem is in thinking that only one of these practices will lead to liberation. As Hui-neng says:

> We should practice straightforwardness and should not attach ourselves to anything. People under delusion believe obstinately in Dharmalaksana [things and form] and so they are stubborn in having their own way of interpreting the "*samādhi* of Specific Mode," which they define as "sitting quietly and continuously without letting any idea arise in the mind." Such an interpretation would rank us with inanimate objects, and is a stumbling block to the right Path which must be kept open. (Price 1969, p. 43)

Hui-neng's point is that Buddhist practice may actually stand in the way of liberation if it is defined too narrowly as "seated meditation." He suggests that it is better to keep the Buddhist "Path" open, and is why he reinterprets *ch'an* meditation in formless terms such as "non-abiding," "non-thinking," and "non-action," which, as Peter Gregory notes, "leaves open the question of what one actually *does* when one meditates" (Gregory 1986, p. 3). Even the distinction between "gradual" and "sudden" awakening, says Hui-neng, should not be reified since they only refer to two types of practices set up for different sentient beings:

> What is meant by "gradual" and "sudden?" The Dharma itself is the same, but in seeing it there is a slow way and a fast way. Seen slowly, it is the gradual; seen fast it is the sudden [teaching]. Dharma is without sudden or gradual, but some people are keen and others dull; hence the names "sudden" and "gradual." (Yampolsky 1967, p. 163)

While it is true that Hui-neng favors the "sudden" approach and disparages the "gradual" as "dull-witted," it is clear from what he says above that there really is no "gradual" or "sudden" approach since both depend on the karmic levels of sentient beings.

The Ch'an Master Lin-chi

A similar issue of the dangers involved in becoming attached to Buddhist praxis is expressed in the *Lin-chi lu*, a small volume of "collected sayings" of the ninth-century Chinese Ch'an master Lin-chi I-hsuan (Japanese Rinzai). Like most Ch'an texts, it purports to contain the basic philosophical and religious message of Buddhism. However, none of this is given to us through any lengthy discussions on the nature of "emptiness," enlightenment, dependent arising, or causal conditioning. Instead, the text repeats these points through the dynamic encounters between Master Lin-chi and his students.

A few important themes related to Lin-chi's style of teaching deserve special attention. First, Lin-chi openly rejects the importance of studying Buddhist doctrine by telling his students that nothing can be gained by reflecting on the Buddha, the nature of enlightenment, or anything else having to do with Buddhist instruction. In fact, Lin-chi tells his students that, quite simply, Buddhist doctrine is a "sham":

> Followers of the Way, there is no Buddha to be gained, and the Three Vehicles, the five natures, the teachings of the perfect and immediate enlightenment are all simply medicines to cure diseases of the moment. None have any true reality. Even if they had, they would still all be mere shams, placards proclaiming superficial matters, so many words lined up, pronouncements of such kind. (Watson 1993, p. 76)

Lin-chi repeats these sentiments to his students throughout the text, telling them that the teachings of the Buddha and Patriarchs "have no special meaning," that "there are no great number of principles to be grasped," that the teachings contained in the sūtras are merely "expositions of surface matters," and that even if one could discover some "special meaning" in all the Buddhist teachings put together, "it would all be names, words, phrases, medicine to apply to the ills of little children to placate them, words dealing with mere surface matters" (Watson 1993, p. 72). Although it may appear that Lin-chi is discarding traditional Buddhist doctrine to establish his own philosophical position, this is not the case, for he tells us that he does not have "a particle of Dharma to give to anyone" (Watson 1993, p. 53).

To take these comments seriously means that we should be cautious about interpreting Lin-chi's project metaphysically: that is, he literally has no Dharma, no philosophical doctrine, and no metaphysical teachings to offer his students. "Everything I am saying to you" he tells them, "is for the moment only, medicine to cure the disease" (Watson 1993, p. 34).

Given that Lin-chi is a respected Ch'an master, however, then what, specifically, does he teach? In trying to answer this question we find ourselves embroiled in a controversy in Ch'an scholarship that will not be settled here. But a few things need to be said. Lin-chi tells his students that his teachings are not doctrinal because what he has to teach has nothing to do with "words and phrases" and is performed "outside the scriptures." For many scholars this is because Lin-chi's teachings are esoteric, non-discursive, and beyond the ken of logic. That is, Lin-chi does not teach in "words and phrases" because he recognizes the inherent limitations of linguistic and conceptual use, and his job as a teacher is to shock his students out of their "dualistic" thinking by using non-conceptual, irrational, and paradoxical means. While this is one popular interpretation of the text, it is also leads us away from the direct form of pedagogy that Lin-chi embodies. To understand this point it might be helpful to imagine the example of a philosophy professor who walks into class one day without any intention of saying a word about the history of philosophy, metaphysics, epistemology, or logic, and who tells his students to put away their notebooks because he is not going to say anything about "philosophy." Thus, there will be no discussion on Kant, Plato, Hume, propositional logic, or the nature of consciousness because, he says, their educational development has nothing to do with such topics. Obviously confused, the students ask, "Then what are we going to do?"

Whereas the average teacher would become highly anxious in this situation, it is exactly this type of environment that Lin-chi thrives in, and is what makes his pedagogy so exciting. He refuses to preach any "doctrine" because spiritual transformation takes place through a direct confrontation between master and disciple. "Doctrine" and what somebody else proclaims are merely "coatings," "placards," and "so many words lined up" that mediate the direct form of pedagogy that Lin-chi sees as vital to transformation.

Lin-chi's students are obviously different from the average college student, and so what arises in his context without "words and phrases" is probably not an issue in a philosophy class. Unlike most college students, Lin-chi's disciples are living within a monastic community and striving for spiritual enlightenment. Lin-chi's manner of addressing their concerns is to respond to their concrete situation, to who they are as individuals, and to their upbringing and environment. "When someone comes to me," says Lin-chi, "I can tell exactly what he is like. Whatever circumstances he may have come from":

> I sit calmly in my seat, and when followers of the Way come for an interview, I see through them all. How do I do this? Because my way of looking at them is different. I don't worry whether on the outside they are common mortals or sages, or get bogged down in the kind of basic nature they have inside. I just see all the way through them and never make an error. (Watson 1993, p. 30)

As Lin-chi notes, his ability to perceive the various dispositions of his students does not rely on anything special: he is not perceiving anything metaphysical and is not concerned with their inner nature. He simply examines who they are, what they say, and how they question him; and then responds in the most appropriate way:

> If a student of less than middling ability comes to me, I snatch away the environment but leave him his existence. If a student of better than middling ability comes to me, I snatch away both environment and existence. If a student of truly superior ability comes to me, I do not snatch away anything, neither environment, nor existence, nor person. If a student appears whose understanding surpasses all these categories, then I deal with him with my whole body and take no account of his ability. (Watson 1993, p. 58)

What Lin-chi teaches therefore depends on what he thinks his students suffer from. It is their "disease" that directs his response. His pedagogical style changes in relation to the student, and he is therefore free to teach a variety of philosophical and religious standpoints or, as Lin-chi puts it, a variety of "robes": "There is a clean pure robe, there is a no-birth robe, a *bodhi* robe, a nirvāṇa robe, a patriarch robe, a Buddha robe." But all of these, he says, are merely "sounds, names, words, phrases . . . . nothing but changes of robe" (Watson 1993, p. 60). Rather than teaching formal doctrines that have little to do with his students' concrete experiences, Lin-chi molds his pedagogical style into a powerful soteriological tool by confronting his students directly.

There is of course one particular "disease" that Lin-chi is trying to cure in his students, and is why he emphasizes that there is no such thing as the Dharma, the Buddha, enlightenment, *nirvāṇa*, practice, and so forth. This "disease" has to with his students taking the sayings and doctrines of previous Ch'an masters as signifying more than provisional devices. That is, they have become attached to the Dharma as having some special "dark meaning" and, hence, suffer because they cannot discover what it means. They thus ask the traditional questions such as, "What is the meaning of Buddhism?" "Why did Bodhidharma came from the West?" "What is the nature of wisdom?" and think that their liberation depends on discovering the answers to these questions:

> The trouble with students these days is that they seize on words and form their understanding on that basis. In a big notebook they copy down the saying of some worthless old fellow, wrapping it up in three layers, five layers of carrying cloth, not letting anyone else see it, calling it the "Dark Meaning" and guarding it as something precious. What a mistake! Blind fools, what sort of juice do they expect to get out of old dried bones? Fellow believers, you rush around frantically one place and another—what are you looking for, tramping till the soles of your feet are squashed flat? There is no Buddha to be sought, no Way to be carried out, no Dharma to be gained. (Watson 1993, p. 61)

To cure this disease, Lin-chi resorts to all those "extreme" measures that are characteristic of the Lin-chi/Rinzai tradition: He gives them slaps, kicks, punches, "irrational" screams, and paradoxical responses. In the *Lin-chi Lu* such harsh measures have positive results because the student often "gets it" and no longer searches for mysterious solutions to Buddhist doctrine. Lin-chi's ability to provoke an "awareness" in his students does not depend on a metaphysical description of the world, however. He simply responds to his "environment" in an immediate way.

Lin-chi's performative style is also found in Dōgen's idea of "the mutual practice of teacher and student." For Dōgen, the transformative and soteriological dimension of Buddhism is a "face-to-face transmission," an intimate relationship between the master and student that is direct and unmediated, and therefore not reducible to philosophical or religious doctrine:

> The authentic ancestors of all generations have continued face-to-face transmission, disciple seeing teacher, and teacher seeing disciple . . . . It is transmitted from vine to vine without being cut. It is transmitted from eye to eye, with the eye open. It is transmitted from face to face, with the face revealed . . . . It is like pouring water into the ocean and spreading it endlessly, or like transmitting the lamp and allowing it to shine forever. . . . Thus, [a student of the Buddha] bowed formally to the Buddha's face. Śākyamuni Buddha's eyes were reflected in his eyes, and his eyes were reflected in Shakyamuni Buddha's eyes. This is the buddha eye; this is the buddha face. It has been transmitted face to face without a generation's gap. (Tanahashi 1985, p. 177)

Dōgen's comments express a fascination with a style of Buddhist pedagogical praxis: a style that is direct and unmediated, a "face-to-face" encounter where compassion and liberation are dynamic and situated firmly in the present. It is, in the words of Hui-neng, "a special transmission outside the scriptures," where spiritual transformation occurs in a relationally liberated "space" in-between the Buddha, the "authentic ancestors," the teacher, and the disciple.

Nāgārjuna and Lin-chi

It is important to pause for a moment and reflect on the similarities between Lin-chi and Nāgārjuna. First, Lin-chi's remarks that there is "no Buddha, no Dharma, no Nirvāṇa, and no Enlightenment" are foreshadowed in Chapter XXV: 24 of Nāgārjuna's *Mādhyamikakārikā* when he says:

> No Dharma was taught by the Buddha
> At any time, in any place, to any person. (Garfield 1995, p. 76)

The similarities between Lin-chi and Nāgārjuna are more apparent when we remember that the *Mādhyamikakārikā* is an attack on traditional Buddhism. As was discussed in the previous chapter, Nāgārjuna covers all the major topics in Buddhist philosophy—causality, the *skandhas*, suffering, the Four Noble Truths, and *nirvāṇa*—and concludes that all of them are "empty," like "dreams" and "illusions, like a city of Gandharvas." One who grasps the view that the *Tathāgata* exists, he says, "having seized the Buddha, constructs conceptual fabrications." Such comments are remarkably similar to Lin-chi's views, as when he says:

> I tell you, there is no Buddha, no Dharma, no practice, no enlightenment. You go off like this on side roads, trying to find something. Blind Fools! (Watson 1993, p. 53)

Second, Lin-chi's assertion that even he does not have "a particle of Dharma to give anyone" is analogous to Nāgārjuna's famous phrase in the *Vigrahavyāvartanī* where he states that he has no philosophical propositions whatsoever. Arguing mainly against the Nyāya position, that says that because Nāgārjuna is asserting the "emptiness" of all things then this must apply to his own assertion as well, he says: "If I had a proposition, this defect would attach to me. But I have no proposition. Therefore I am not at fault" (Bhattacharya 1978, p. 23). While the meaning of this passage is disputed among Mādhyamika scholars, let it suffice for the moment to say that, like Lin-chi, Nāgārjuna is not advancing any metaphysical view or theory.

And third, just as Lin-chi's pedagogical method depends on "contradictory" teachings, so Nāgārjuna often uses what seem like paradoxical statements to get his points across. In his *Mādhyamikakārikā* (18:6 and 18:8), for example, he says the following:

> The Buddhas have made known the conception of self and taught the doctrine of no-self. At the same time, they have not spoken of something as the self or as the non-self. (Kalupahana 1986, p. 267)

> Everything is such, not such, both such and not such, and neither such and not such: this is the Buddha's admonition. (Kalupahana 1986, p. 269)

Such "contradictory" teachings are not unlike Lin-chi's style which, depending on the student, will either snatch away the "person," the "environment," both, or neither, and which freely utilizes a variety of philosophical and religious "robes." Unlike Nāgārjuna, however, Lin-chi often resorts to more "extreme" measures.

> If they come with a raised hand, I hit the raised hand; if they come mouthing something, I hit them in the mouth; if they come making motions with their eyes, I hit them in the eye. (Watson 1993, p. 53)

Now it should be recalled that Lin-chi has a reason for revealing this aspect of this pedagogical "robe." That is, when he is making these comments he is doing something quite different than slapping someone in the face. His comments are more reflective than performative because he is telling his disciples about his method of teaching. But his reason for doing this is because his students have taken the method for something deeper, something more mysterious and metaphysically real than it actually is. Thus, he seems to be telling them outright in these passages that Buddhist methodology is just this, i.e., no more mysterious than the slapping of a face or the teaching of "contradictory" views. And his reason for practicing such "harsh" measures, he tells them, is to "snatch" something away from them, to confront their "environment" and, like a thief, steal it away.

Nāgārjuna's complaint with the Abhidharma traditions should be seen in a similar light. Like Lin-chi's "thief," Nāgārjuna is trying to "steal" something from the Abhidharma philosophers. In their desire for liberation they have become attached to the teachings, and have therefore missed the most significant teaching in Buddhism: non-attachment. To confront this "illness," Nāgārjuna resorts to "skill-in-means" and uses their own way of speaking and their own views against them. While it is true that Lin-chi and Nāgārjuna are separated by wide cultural, religious, and philosophical differences, they are both attacking a similar issue of attachment and highlighting the problem—which is long-standing in Buddhist history—of becoming attached to the practices of non-attachment. And it is to counter this problem that Nāgārjuna says—along with the entire Mahāyāna tradition—that "emptiness is the unsurpassed medicine" of non-attachment (Lindtner 1986, p. 29), and that even this very "emptiness" is "empty."

Pure Land Buddhism

Any discussion of *upāya* would be incomplete without some reference to the Pure Land tradition. This may seem odd coming within a discussion on Ch'an since the two traditions seem diametrically opposed. Pure Land Buddhism emphasizes the limited intellectual and spiritual capacities of human beings, says that enlightenment can be achieved through faith in an "external power" (Chinese *t'o-li*; Japanese *tariki*), and claims that by reciting the name of Amida Buddha one will be reborn in the Western Pure Land. Ch'an, on the other hand, affirms the unique character of the human mind, and is critical of any distinction between the present moment and a future paradise, sentient beings and divinity, or religious practice and enlightenment. Whereas Pure Land emphasizes faith in an external source, Ch'an relies on the human mind's own ability to overcome its inadequacies.

While it is true that Ch'an and Pure Land offer divergent religious views and practices, however, they also exist side by side. This is especially the case in China where Pure Land chanting is balanced by Ch'an meditation, and where one can find a meditation hall and a recitation hall existing side by side in the same monastery. When John Blofeld traveled to the famous Nan Hua Monastery in China, for instance, he witnessed Ch'an monks performing rites before an altar of Amida Buddha. Thinking he was in a "pure" Ch'an monastery that is opposed to theistic beliefs and devotional practices, he asked the abbott of the monastery why the monks were worshiping Amida. The abbott's reply was, "Why not? It is like every other Zen monastery in China. Why should it be different? Hundreds of years ago there were many sects, but the teachings have long been synthesized—which is how it should be" (Blofeld 1959, p. 88).

Chinese historians are now aware that the synthesis between the two traditions came about mainly from political pressure and the need to integrate different Buddhist traditions. However, Pure Land thinkers facilitated the union by criticizing early Ch'an Buddhists for adopting an esoteric and elitist orthodoxy. While Hui-neng and Shen-hsiu debated over methodology, and while Lin-chi severely reprimanded his students for being attached to Buddhism, Pure-Land thinkers attacked Ch'an for its own brand of attachment. As Tz'u-min Hui-jih says:

> Various practices are broadly taught in the scriptures as a cause for becoming a Buddha, not merely the Six Perfections. How can Ch'an masters be so strongly attached to meditative concentration [*ch'an-ting*] as the correct cause of Buddhahood, and not [realize the importance of] the remaining perfections? (Gregory 1986, p. 169)

The problem with some of the early Ch'an Buddhists, according to Pure Land thinkers such as Hui-jih, is that they distort the teachings in the scriptures by saying that Ch'an practice is the only "gate" to enlightenment, when in fact the *Prajñāpāramitā* teaches "Six Perfections" and "ten thousand practices" (Chappell 1986, p. 173). In doing this, they neglect the *upāyic* thrust of Buddhism by emphasizing an esoteric, austere, and exclusive praxis. Shen-hsiu's polishing is reserved for a select few, and one would need to live in a monastery a long time to receive a "liberating blow" from Lin-chi. Even Hui-neng's "immediate" approach, that is supposedly available to "illiterate barbarians," turns out to be a rigorous, monastic life, requiring celibacy and daily meditation. Pure Land Buddhism, on the other hand, is available to everyone, even those with "dull capacities" or with little patience for traditional meditation. The Vietnamese Buddhist Thao-Du'o'ng (eleventh century C.E.) who introduced the union of Ch'an and Pure Land in Vietnam, expresses this point by saying:

> Though you may practice Buddhism in many ways, in summary there are three main methods; meditation, visualization, and Buddha's-name recitation. The method of meditation has no definite way to follow and is therefore a difficult practice. If you do not have an enlightened master or a capable mind, you may stop midway in your progress or remain mistaken for your entire life. Visualization is a very subtle method; without a good teacher or prajna wisdom, complete enlightenment is hard to attain. Buddha's-name recitation is a quick and easy method. In all the ages past both intelli-

> gent and dull, both men and women have been able to practice [it]. Nobody makes a mistake with this method. . . . Putting worries aside, you may therefore proceed with a decisive heart. (Corless 1995, p. 266)

The heart of Pure Land practice rests on the invocation of Amida Buddha's name (*nien-fo*) who, upon hearing it, will immediately come to one's aid. The invocation "*Nan-mo O-mi-t'o Fo*" ("Hail! Amida Buddha!") awakens Amida Buddha's compassion, and will transform the practitioner from fear and suffering to "immeasurable light" and purity. According to the Japanese Pure Land Buddhist Honen, the mere invocation of Amida's name, whether walking, standing still, sitting, or lying down, is all that is required to attain liberation:

> The method of salvation that I have propounded is neither a sort of meditation, such as been practiced by many scholars in China and Japan, nor is it a repetition of the Buddha's name by those who have studied and understood the deep meaning of it. It is nothing but the mere repetition of the "*Namu Amida Butsu,*" without a doubt of His mercy, whereby one may be born into the Land of Perfect Bliss . . . . Thus (one) should fervently practice the repetition of the name Amida, and that alone. (De Barry 1969 p. 331)

Amida Buddha is invoked as "Other Power" (*t'o-li*) because Pure Land recognizes that not everyone is capable of relying on themselves for liberation. Amida is therefore described as a deity with an infinite abundance of compassion who extends his ray of light upon saints and sinners alike.

One need only invoke his name or contemplate a Pure Land of "infinite bliss" to attain spiritual transformation.

While such theological and devotional elements may sound completely non-Buddhist, especially if one thinks of "pure" Buddhism in terms of "non-self," "emptiness," and "one-pointed concentration" (*samādhi*), Pure Land thinkers see themselves fully within the basic teachings and practices of traditional Buddhist thought, and see Nāgārjuna as one of their first Patriarchs. As Nāgārjuna says in the *Daśabhūmikavibhāṣā Śāstra*:

> To discipline oneself in deeds of austerity is difficult; whereas to proceed by means of faith is easy . . . . Those who wish to reach the stage of non-retrogression quickly should have a mind filled with reverence and pronounce the Buddha-name, always keeping it in mind. (Williams 1989, p. 257)

According to Pure Land thinkers, the Dharma contains "other power" and "self power," and, depending on the spiritual levels and karmic disposition of human beings, both teachings are effective. The problem is in thinking only one of these teachings is "true" Buddhism, or, like Shen-hsiu, that there is only one soteriological guide for everyone. This form of attachment denies liberation to all those "lower" beings and, more importantly, destroys the message of compassion that is central to all of the Buddha's teachings. Amida's compassion, on the other hand, extends to everyone. Like Śākyamuni who saw the world as multi-colored lotuses, Amida experiences the different karmic levels of human beings and understands that no single teaching is sufficient to encompass them all. His "infinite light" shines on everyone, illuminating numerous paths for those who are in most need of a compassionate response.

Summary

Taken together, the Ch'an and Pure Land traditions reveal two aspects of *upāya* that have been emphasized throughout this study. On the hand, there is the iconoclastic resistance of Ch'an denouncing all forms of Buddhist attachment and reification by claiming that there is no Buddha, no Dharma, no practice, and no enlightenment. This critical aspect of *upāya* repeats itself throughout history: in Vimalakīrti's condemnation against those who "preach without knowing the thoughts and inclinations of others;" in Nāgārjuna's attack on the *dharmas*; and in the Buddha's reproach to his disciples, "if you cling to it (the Dharma), if you fondle it, if you treasure it, if you are attached to it, then you do not understand that the teaching is similar to a raft." Ch'an's anti-methodological side—exemplified in Lin-chi's "shout" and Hui-neng's sudden enlightenment—is the continuation of this critical tradition.

But *upāya* is not only negative and critical. It also signifies what Peter Hershock calls "liberating intimacy," that is, a unique pedagogical encounter that is suffused with immediacy, spontaneity, and compassion. Amida's relationship with the world brings out this positive side to *upāya*, and shows that a bodhisattva's wisdom (*prajñā*) is identical to compassion (*karuṇā*). "The actualization of the Buddha's Great Compassion and the witness of faith by sentient beings," says Nishitani Keiji, "are seen to be really one, a single realization" (Nishitani 1982, p. 27). This "realization," in which wisdom and compassion are inseparable, is the "twining vines" of enlightenment where the Buddha sees disciple, and disciple sees the Buddha. That the Ch'an tradition in China—so famous for its antinomianism and self-reliance—claims Pure Land "other-power" enlightenment as its own shows a deep commitment to an *upāyic* philosophy that began with the Buddha's first "Turning of the Wheel."

Conclusion

The development of *upāya* in the history of Buddhism spans over two millennia and covers many different Buddhist traditions throughout the world. While it originated in the Buddha's enlightenment experience and his proclamation to teach Dharma, it was not until Buddhism crossed over into China and Japan that *upāya* fully blossomed into a rich philosophical system. There is therefore still much to learn from the doctrine of *upāya*, both from the traditional Sanskrit and Pāli sources, and from the living Buddhist traditions throughout East and Southeast Asia.

The goal of this book is to show how *upāya* directs our attention to the efficacy of Buddhist praxis and to the problems associated with justifying a fixed practice for all people. The issue is not only whether any particular practice works, but whether it is possible—from a Buddhist perspective—to establish normative guidelines for all practitioners. The early Abhidharma tradition is singled out in Chapter 2 as one example of this problem, not because it engaged in metaphysical reflection, but because it adopted one set of practices—those found in the *abhidharma* texts—and tried to establish them as the *only* "medicinal" guide for all Buddhists. *Upāya* was developed to counter this approach, and thinkers like Nāgārjuna, Lin-chi, and Dōgen, and texts such as the *Lotus Sūtra* and *Vimalakīrtinirdeśa* use the doctrine of *upāya* to attack those Buddhists who try to establish fixed metapractical criteria. From the perspective of *upāya*, no single teaching or practice is sufficient to cover the vast range of karmic differences in the world, and to think otherwise not only goes against Buddhist doctrine, but distorts the message of compassion that is central to Buddhism.

It is tempting to think that what separates the various Buddhist traditions is conflicting metaphysical positions, or that they are divided over different conceptions of truth, language, causality, and consciousness, and that *upāyic* terms like "emptiness," *dharmas*, the "two truths," and *anātman* are metaphysically charged terms that mirror Western philosophical categories. However, an *upāyic* analysis of Buddhism leads in a different direction altogether. As a specific form of metapraxis, *upāya* is not reflecting on the limits of knowledge, the nature of reality, or metaphysical assertions, but on the efficacy and justifiability of Buddhist praxis. While metaphysics asks us to reflect on general issues in the philosophy of language, truth, consciousness, and causality, metapraxis asks to look at praxis itself, how it works and why. The difference between them is not "theory" versus "practice," since metaphysics theorizes about the nature of the world and metapraxis theorizes specifically about praxis. Rather, the difference is what we are asked to reflect upon. Moreover, metapraxis is not opposed to metaphysics, and does not deny the possible benefits of metaphysical reflection, but simply says that such investigations are of a different order and, in the case of *upāya*, unrelated to the issue of praxis that divides the various Buddhist traditions.

A number of Western scholars lose this critical insight when they discuss Buddhism in relation to metaphysics. The best example of this problem is found in Western interpretations of Nāgārjuna, that see him arguing against epistemological realism, essentialism, causality, linguistic structures, "truth," and rationality, and see him saying that enlightenment requires the deconstruction of our most implicit metaphysical assumptions. According to Murti, for example:

> The dialectic, then, as the *Śūnyatā* of *dṛṣṭis*, is the negation of standpoints, which are the initial negation of the real that is essentially indeterminate. Correctly understood, *Śūnyatā* is not annihilation, but the negation of negation; it is the conscious correction of an initial unconscious falsification of the real. (Murti 1955, p. 271)

Murti not only sees Nāgārjuna diagnosing a fundamental problem in human existence, but sees his dialectical method as the "cure" for all delusion. Since humans supposedly "cover" reality with conceptual thought (which is delusory), we need to reverse this process, and Nāgārjuna's dialectic will cure this. Thus, Murti sees himself offering an *upāyic* account of Buddhism: "emptiness" is the "means" for correcting a "falsification of the real."

Frederick Streng also tries to give an *upāyic* reading of Nāgārjuna. "Emptiness," he says, is the "means for quelling the pain found in existential 'becoming' which results from longing after an eternal undisturbed entity" (Streng 1967, p.149). Whereas Murti says Nāgārjuna helps us achieve liberation by "demolishing" what he calls "the conflict in reason," Streng says Nāgārjuna attacks a referential view of language that posits objective "things" in the world. By understanding a "relational norm of meaning" we will be "cured" of the longing for an "eternal, undisturbed entity." Huntington expresses a similar view when he says:

> Recognition of the strictly contextual or pragmatic significance of the thoughts and objects that populate our

> mental and material world renders meaningless any search for a transcendental ground behind these phenomena . . . . What is immediately given in everyday experience is indeed all that there is, for the inherently interdependent nature of the components of this experience *is* the truth of the highest meaning: both the means to the goal (*mārga; upāya*) and the goal itself (*nirvāṇa*). (Huntington 1989, p. 40)

For Garfield, the *upāyic* element in Nāgārjuna's philosophy lies in showing us the nature of reification, or the tendency to take the "conventional" world for something other than what it is:

> Reification is the root of grasping and craving and hence of all suffering. And it is perfectly natural, despite its incoherence. Nāgārjuna intends one to break this habit and extirpate the root of suffering . . . . Only with the simultaneous realization of the emptiness, but conventional reality, of phenomena and of the emptiness of emptiness, argues Nāgārjuna, can suffering be wholly uprooted. (Garfield 1995, p. 314)

Nāgārjuna's dialectic uproots this tendency to "reify" the world, according to Garfield, and shows that all phenomena are "empty," and that this very "emptiness" is itself "empty." Realizing both, he says, is the "means" to liberation.

It could be argued that such readings suffer from a prejudice that is deeply embedded in the Western philosophical tradition. The fact that "emptiness" refers to metaphysical "beliefs" and propositions, that it says something about how all things are "conventional" by nature, lacking in "essence," or linguistically structured, and that it supposedly "cures" everyone (even those who don't practice Buddhism) of their deepest philosophical ills shows that a decontextualizing process has begun, a process that treats metapractical issues in propositional terms and apart from their cultural and rhetorical context. When we are further advised that liberation is impossible without adopting a certain epistemological framework, or a "belief" about the how the mind works, how causality is linguistically structured, or how all things are conventionally posited, it seems we have left a strictly Buddhist framework and entered one that is distinctly Western.

The problem runs deeper than this, however, since these various metaphysical interpretations see Nāgārjuna as establishing a fixed—albeit metaphysical—path. Whether the problem is "falsifying the real," a "referential view of language," "essentialism," or "reification," Nāgārjuna is depicted as speaking universally: he not only diagnoses an innate "sickness" in human nature, but cures it by prescribing a set remedy, i.e., "emptiness." However, both the problem and the cure on these accounts are totalizing and essentialistic. Asserted independently of any rhetorical context and apart from the karmic dispositions of individuals, they are expressed with the assumption that there is a single cause to *all* human suffering and a single cure. It is not simply that Nāgārjuna does metaphysics, but that he thinks metaphysical reflection is necessary for enlightenment. While this approach may appear *upāyic*, it embodies the type of "poisonous" remedies that *upāya* rejects. In other words, it is bad "medicine."

If we examine Nāgārjuna's philosophy within the context of metapraxis, however, then we see him operating within a Buddhist tradition that argues against the imposition of *any* fixed criteria when it comes to overcoming suffering or achieving enlightenment. His *upāyic* dialectic of "emptiness" undercuts the philosophical justifications of the Abhidharma tradition, and, rather than asserting "emptiness" as a new totalizing practice, he tells us that even "emptiness" is "empty." Whereas the Abhidharma philosophers sought to impose fixed standards for all Buddhist practitioners, Nāgārjuna argues for the "emptiness" of praxis and for the "emptiness of emptiness." In doing so, he effectively undermines the desire to become attached to "emptiness" or reify it into a new fixed soteriological path (*mārga*). The point of his *upāyic* critique is not to establish new absolute metapractical criteria, but to question whether any such criteria are necessary when it comes to achieving enlightenment, responding to suffering, or cultivating compassion. While this may presuppose certain assumptions about the nature of the world, human beings, and spiritual efficacy, it is doubtful that he is engaged in a metaphysical critique, and even more doubtful that he is trying to establish fixed metapractical criteria. The Western interpretations of Nāgārjuna not only miss this critical insight when they place his philosophy within a metaphysical discourse, but effectively undermine the *upāyic* nature of his philosophy by interpreting "emptiness" as a fixed soteriological guide that appeals to all people under all circumstances.

This does not mean that *upāya* leads to relativism, or that it adopts a pragmatic criterion of "truth." Rather, it is critical of establishing any fixed criteria—be it relativism, pragmatism, or otherwise—when it comes to addressing the concrete, embodied suffering of others. The bodhisattva exemplifies this non-attached perspective by refusing to "course in" or fixate upon any single praxis, and by resisting all soteriological "marks," "signs," and fixed doctrines. He rejects the imposition of fixed metapractical criteria—not because he thinks the use of criteria are always wrong—but because he is committed to the expression of compassion and to the belief that attachment to any single practice, teaching, or doctrine stands in the way responding to those who suffer. What Dōgen calls the "face-to-face transmission," in which teacher sees disciple, and disciple sees teacher, is a bodhisattvic exchange that is direct and unmediated, relying on no fixed criteria and no substantial doctrines, and in which liberation is revealed as intimacy and love of another. *Upāya* reflects this unmediated encounter, showing that spiritual transformation occurs in a liberated "space" where one's body and mind is fully present, and where the sheer "emptiness" of anything fixed or tangible leads to a deep sense of vulnerability and intimacy. "A Bodhisattva," says the *Prajñāpāramitā*, "does not review any dharma. In consequence he does not tremble, is not frightened, nor terrified. No dharma can cow his mind, and he knows no regrets . . . . It is thus that a Bodhisattva, who courses in perfect wisdom, not having settled down in all-dharmas, grows in the perfection of giving" (Conze 1975a, p. 92–94). That we should understand this as a metaphysical issue leads us away from a soteriology based on a "face-to-face" encounter.

After having attacked so many others for turning Buddhism into "bad medicine," however, and after having devoted an entire book to explaining how it is impossible to make sense of skillful means apart from the concrete needs and karmic dispositions of an audience, the position of this study is obviously problematic. Is this book an *upāya*? Is it grounded in the lives of others, a practical guide or "raft" toward liberation? If it is true that skillful means is a practical guide, and that by thinking of it apart from praxis we lose sight of what Buddhism is all about, then have I not committed the "fallacy" of offering an abstract view of *upāya*?

These questions expose the weakest point in this entire study. This book was not meant to be a "raft" or a path toward liberation. It is not grounded in the life of Buddhist practice; nor is it a meditation tool. Therefore, it too is guilty of speaking about Buddhism apart from practice, and suffers from the problem of explaining its central ideas (e.g., *upāya*) apart from how they function in the lives of Buddhist practitioners. Moreover, in privileging *upāya* as the central concept in Buddhist thought, I have succumbed to the type of attachment that the Buddha, Vimalakīrti, Nāgārjuna, and Lin-chi all fought against.

On the other hand, what distinguishes this book from those criticized is that it was not intended as an *upāya*. The preceding arguments did not determine in advance what any path is, how liberation should be achieved, or how to overcome suffering. Rather, they tried to remain faithful to an *upāyic* philosophy that undercuts our ability to say in advance—and previous to knowing who one is addressing or what one's "illness" is—how liberation should be achieved. This is where this study differs most from those criticized. For most Western scholars, Nāgārjuna's doctrine of "emptiness" is a panacea, a medicine that will cure everyone regardless of the disease, and their interpretations are generally devoted to telling us what our problem is, and how to cure it. And all of this, oddly enough, without even knowing who we are. This book argues why this approach "tends not to edification," and tries to express Vimalakīrti's lesson to Pūrṇa: "The disciples who do not know the thoughts or the inclinations of others are not able to teach the Dharma to anyone" (Thurman 1986, p. 29).

References

Bhattacharya, Kamaleswar (1978), *The Dialectical Method of Nāgārjuna*. Delhi: Motilal Banarsidass.

Blofeld, John (1959), *The Wheel of Life*. London: Rider and Company.

Burt, E. A., ed. (1955), *The Teachings of the Compassionate Buddha*. New York: New American Library.

Buswell, Robert, Jr., and Robert Gimello (1992), *Paths to Liberation*. Honolulu: University of Hawai`i Press.

Chappell, David W. (1986), "From Dispute to Dual Cultivation: Pure Land Responses to Ch'an Critics," in *Traditions of Meditation in Chinese Buddhism*. Honolulu: University of Hawai`i Press.

Cheng, Hsueh-li, trans. (1982), *Nāgārjuna's "Twelve Gate Treatise."* Boston: D. Reidel.

Conze, Edward (1954), *Buddhist Texts Through the Ages*. New York: Philosophical Library, Inc.

——— (1956), *Buddhist Meditation*. London: George Allen & Unwin, Ltd.

——— (1967), *Buddhist Thought in India*. Ann Arbor: University of Michigan Press.

——— (1968), "Mahayana Buddhism," in *Thirty Years of Buddhist Studies*. Columbia, S. C.: University of South Carolina Press.

——— (1973), *Perfect Wisdom: The Short Prajnaparamita Texts*. Leicester: Buddhist Publishing Group.

——— (1975a), *Buddhism: Its Essence and Development*. New York: Harper and Row.

——— (1975b), *The Large Sutra on Perfect Wisdom*. Los Angeles: University of California Press.

Corless, Roger, J. (1995), "Pure Land Piety," in *Buddhist Spirituality*. New York: The Crossroad Publishing Company.

Coward, Harold (1990), *Derrida and Indian Philosophy*. Albany: State University of New York Press.

De Barry, William Theodore (1972), *The Buddhist Tradition in India, China, and Japan*. New York: Vintage Books.

Della Santina, Peter (1986), *Madhyamaka Schools in India*. Delhi: Motilal Banarsidass.

Dumoulin, Heinrich, S. J. (1963), *A History of Zen Buddhism*. Boston: Beacon Press.

——— (1988), *Zen Buddhism: A History, Vol. 1, India and China*. New York: Macmillian Publishing Company.

——— (1990), *Zen Buddhism: A History, Vol. 2, Japan*. New York: Macmillian Publishing Company.

Garfield, Jay (1990), "Epoche and Sunyata: Skepticism East and West," *Philosophy East and West*, Vol. 40, p. 285–307.

——— (1995), *The Fundamental Wisdom of the Middle Way: Nāgārjuna's Mulamadhyamakakārikā*. New York: Oxford University Press.

Garner, Richard (1993), "Are Convenient Fictions Harmful to Your Health?" *Philosophy East and West*, Vol. 43, p. 362–395.

Gregory, Peter, N. (1986), *Traditions of Meditation in Chinese Buddhism*. Honolulu: University of Hawai`i Press.

Griffiths, Paul J. (1986), *On Being Mindless: Buddhist Meditation and the Mind-Body Problem*. LaSalle, Ill: Open Court.

Gudmunsen, Chris (1977), *Wittgenstein and Buddhism*. New York: Harper and Row

Guenther, Herbert V. (1976), *Philosophy and Psychology in the Abhidharma*. Boston: Shambhala Publications, Inc.

Hershock, Peter, D. (1996), *Liberating Intimacy: Enlightenment and Social Virtuosity in Ch'an Buddhism*. Albany: State University of New York Press.

Hirakawa, Akira (1990), *A History of Indian Buddhism: From Sakyamuni to Early Mahayana*, Paul Groner, trans. Honolulu: University of Hawai`i Press.

Horner, I. B., trans. (1962), *Book of Disciplines*. London: Luzac & Co.

———trans. (1967), *The Middle Length Sayings I*. London: Luzac & Co.

Huntington, C. W. Jr. (1989), *The Emptiness of Emptiness: An Introduction to Early Indian Madhyamika*. Honolulu: University of Hawai`i Press.

Inada, Kenneth (1970), *Nāgārjuna: A Translation of His Mulamadhyamakakārikā with an Introductory Essay*. Tokyo: The Hokuseido Press.

James, William (1936), *The Varieties of Religious Experience*. New York: The Modern Library Edition.

Jayatilleke, K. N. (1963), *Early Buddhist Theory of Knowledge*. London: George Allen & Unwin.

Kalupahana, David (1975), *Causality: The Central Philosophy of Buddhism*. Honolulu: The University Press of Hawai`i

——— (1976), *Buddhist Philosophy: A Historical Analysis*. Honolulu: University of Hawai`i Press.

——— (1986), *Nāgārjuna: The Philosophy of the Middle Way*. Albany: State University of New York Press.

Kasulis, Thomas P. (1992), "Philosophy as Metapraxis," in *Discourse and Practice*. Frank Reynolds and David Tracy, eds. Albany: State University of New York Press.

Katz, Nathan (1981), "Nāgārjuna and Wittgenstein on Error," in *Buddhist and Western Philosophy*. Nathan Katz, ed. New Delhi: Sterling.

Kern, Hendrik, trans. (1963), *Saddharma-Pundarika: Or the Lotus of the True Law. Sacred Book of the East*, Vol. 21. New York: Dover Press.

Lang, Karen, trans. (1986), *Catuhsataka*. Copenhagen: Akademisk Forlag.

Laycock, Stephen (1994), *Mind as Mirror and Mirroring the Mind: Buddhist Reflections on Western Phenomenology*. Albany: State University of New York Press.

Lindtner, Christian (1986), *Masters of Wisdom*. California: Dharma Publishing.

Loy, David (1985), "The Paradox of Causality in Madhyamika," *International Philosophical Quarterly*, Vol. 25, p. 63–72.

———(1987), "The Cloture of Deconstruction: A Mahayana Critique of Derrida," *International Philosophical Quarterly*, Vol. 27, p. 59-80.

Mahathera, Nyanatiloka (1983), *Guide Through The Abhidhamma-Pitaka*. Kandy: Sri Lanka Buddhist Publication Society.

Matilal, B. M. (1986), *Perception: An Essay in Classical Indian Theories of Knowledge*. New York: Oxford University Press.

Matsunaga, Alicia (1974), "The Concept of *Upaya* in Mahayana Buddhist Philosophy," *Japanese Journal of Religious Studies*, Vol. 1, p. 51-72.

Murti, T.R.V. (1955), *The Central Philosophy of Buddhism.* London: George Allen & Unwin Ltd.

Nagao, Gadjin M. (1991), *Madhayamika and Yogacara.* Albany: State University of New York.

Nehamas, Alexander (1985), *Nietzsche: Life as Literature,* Cambridge: Harvard University Press.

Nietzsche, Frederick (1969), *On The Genealogy of Morals.* Walter Kaufmann, trans., New York: Vintage Books.

———(1974), *The Gay Science.* Walter Kaufmann trans., New York: Vintage Books.

———(1989), *Beyond Good and Evil.* Walter Kaufmann trans., New York: Vintage Books.

Organ, Troy (1954), "The Silence of the Buddha," *Philosophy East and West,* Vol. 4, p. 121–141.

Pruden, Leo M., trans. (1988-1990), Vasabandhu's *Abhidharmakosabhasyam,* from French trans. by Louis de la Vallee Poussin. Freemont, Calif.: Asian Humanities Press.

Pye, Michael, (1978), *Skilful Means: A Concept in Mahayana Buddhism.* London: Gerald Duckworth & Co. Ltd.

Radhakrishnan, S. A. (1973), *Sourcebook in Indian Philosophy.* Princeton: Princeton University Press.

Rahula, Walpola (1974), *What the Buddha Taught.* New York: Grove Press, Inc.

Raju, P. T. (1985), *Structural Depths of Indian Thought.* Albany: State University of New York Press.

Rhys-Davids, T. W., trans. (1899), *Dialogues of the Buddha: Sacred Books of the Buddhists,* Vol. II. London: Oxford University Press.

Robinson, Richard (1967), *Early Madhyamika in India and China.* Madison: Wisconsin Press.

——— (1972), "Did Nāgārjuna Really Refute all Metaphysical Views?" *Philosophy East and West*, Vol. 22. p. 121–125.

——— (1977), "Some Logical Aspects of Nāgārjuna's System," *Philosophy East and West*, Vol. 27. p. 110–117.

Rorty, Richard (1980), *Philosophy and the Mirror of Nature*. Princeton: Princeton University Press.

Ruegg, David S. (1981), *The Literature of the Mādhyamika School of Philosophy in India*. Wiesbaden: Otto Harrassowitz.

Russell, Bertrand (1985), *The Philosophy of Logical Atomism*. LaSalle, Ill: Open Court.

Siderits, Mark (1988), "Nāgārjuna as Anti-Realist," *Journal of Indian Philosophy*, Vol. 16. p. 97–125.

——— (1989), "Thinking on Empty: Madhyamaka Anti-Realism and Canons of Rationality," in *Rationality in Question*, Shlomo Biderman, ed. E. J. Brill, Leiden.

Sprung, Mervyn, trans. (1979), *Lucid Exposition of the Middle Way*. Boulder: Prajna Press.

Stcherbatsky, Fyodor (1923), *Buddhist Logic*, Vol. 1. Leningrad: Academy of Sciences of the USSR.

——— (1961), *The Central Philosophy of Buddhism*, New Delhi: India: Susil Gupta, Ltd.

——— (1968), *The Conception of Buddhist Nirvana*. New Delhi: Motilal Banarsidass.

Streng, Frederick (1967), *Emptiness: A Study in Religious Meaning*. Nashville: Abingdon Press.

Stryk, Lucian (1968), *World of the Buddha*. New York: Grove Press.

Suzuki, D. T. (1956), *Zen Buddhism: Selected Writings*. New York: Doubleday Anchor Books.

Tanahashi, Kazuaki (1985), *Moon in a Dewdrop: Writings of Zen Master Dōgen*. New York: North Point Press.

Tatz, Mark (1994), *The Skill in Means Sutra*. New Delhi: Motilal Banarsidass.

Thurman, Robert (1980), "Philosophical Nonegocentrism in Wittgenstein and Candrakirti in their Treatment of the Private Language Problem," *Philosophy East and West*, Vol. 30. p. 86–101.

———(1986), *The Holy Teachings of Vimalakīrti*. University Park: The Pennsylvania State University Press.

Trungpa, Chogyam (1978), *Glimpses of Abhidharma: From a Seminar on Buddhist Psychology*. Boulder: Prajna Press.

Tuck, Andrew (1990), *Comparative Philosophy and the Philosophy of Scholarship*. New York: Oxford University Press.

Waddell, Norman, trans. (1973), "The Zen Sermons of Bankei Yotaku" *Eastern Buddhist*, 6.2. p. 62–89.

Warder, A. K. (1973), "Is Nāgārjuna a Mahayanist?" in *The Problem of Two Truths in Buddhism and Vedanta*, Mervyn Sprung, ed. Boston: D. Reidel.

Warren, Henry Clarke (1986), *Buddhism in Translations*, Harvard Oriental Series, Vol. III. Cambridge: Harvard University Press.

Watson, Burton, trans. (1993), *The Zen Teachings of the Master Lin-chi*. Boston: Shambhala.

Williams, Paul (1989), *Mahayana Buddhism: The Doctrinal Foundations*. London: Routledge.

Wittgenstein, Ludwig (1953), *Tractatus Logico-Philosophicus*, B. F. McGuinness, trans. London: Routledge & Kegan Paul.

Wood, Thomas (1994), *Nagarjunian Disputations: A Philosophical Journey Through an Indian Looking Glass*. Honolulu: University of Hawai`i Press.

Yampolsky, Philip, B., trans. (1967), *The Platform Sutra of the Sixth Pattriarch*. New York: Columbia University Press.

Index